A Tail of Grace

A Year in Search of Home
after the Death of my Soul-Dog

By Ashley Brown

MEZCALITA
PRESS

MEZCALITA
PRESS

MEZCALITA PRESS, LLC
Norman, Oklahoma

A Tail of Grace

A Year in Search of Home
after the Death of My Soul-Dog

By Ashley Brown

This book is dedicated to Cayenne, my soul-dog,
and all animal souls—the wild ones; the ones
I've known and loved for a little while; and
Stoney, Dylan, and Lacey.

Table of Contents

Author's Note

"Grace" has more official definitions than most words in the dictionary. My personal definition, or concept, of grace supersedes words. It's something you know and feel when you see it or experience it. Borrowing from all those dictionary definitions, though, I'd say it has a lot to do with kindness, acceptance, generosity, divinity, love, and mercy. Many of the definitions of grace refer to God, as in "an influence emanating from God and acting for the spiritual well-being of the recipient." Replace "God" with "Spirit," or "Universe," and that comes pretty close, for me.

The story "Laced with Grace" was previously published by spiritualityhealth.com.

"We know that sooner or later our physical bodies will no longer exist. We only have a few sunrises, a few sunsets, a few full moons that we can enjoy. This is our time to be alive, to be fully present, to enjoy ourselves, to enjoy one another."

~ Don Miguel Ruiz and Don Jose Ruiz,
The Fifth Agreement

A Tail of Grace

By Ashley Brown

MEZCALITA
PRESS

The Decision
August 27, 2020

In the middle of the night last night…as I lay on the floor trying to comfort Cayenne, while she whimpered in the corner of the bedroom—pawing aimlessly as if trying to escape the walls of this physical world—I decided it was time. I'd make the appointment in the morning.

Just over a month ago, we celebrated fifteen years together. I adopted her when I was twenty-five. I barely remember who I was before her, and I'm afraid I don't know who I am now without her. I'm terrified of what the world will feel like thirty hours from now. I'm reminding myself that this cannot be avoided—there is no "right time" when this will hurt any less. Making this decision for her is not something I wanted to do. I thought I could manifest a peaceful transition for her, when she would just go to sleep for the last time. But last night, she was crying out for help. Though she is not sick, her systems are shutting down. She is weak and uncomfortable, and she doesn't have the strength to go where she needs to go on her own. She doesn't have the will to eat. When she is awake, she continually walks into walls, furniture, shrubs, and trees. She's trying to go…so I have to help her. I have to send her off and out of her body.

I have to know—not believe, but *know*—that when she is free of her form, she won't really be gone. Olivia Hawker's book *One for the Blackbird, One for the Crow* contains some beautiful passages about death. I've never been able to put into words (or even coherent thoughts) what I think happens when we die. I don't adhere to any religious traditions—or concepts of heaven and hell—that oversimplify something we cannot actually fathom. But I've never doubted that energy doesn't actually die when the physical bodies that temporarily carry it do. The narrator of that novel is an intuitive thirteen-year-old girl who sees and understands what most of us can't.

When they butcher the chickens on the family ranch, she sees their "quick, curious, darting little spirits bursting like sparks from a campfire, dispersing out into the world." She goes on to say, "My ma had cherished a pet cat some years ago, and when it had died suddenly, I sat beside its body and felt the cat's awareness linger for half an hour or more. The cat had been amazed by its sudden weightlessness, pleasantly drawn to all the silver strands of light that reached for it, thirsty for its spirit—the threads of all the lives that continued on: mine and my family's and the hens in the yard and the cattle in their pen, the squash vines and carrots in the garden, the insects trilling on the prairie—the prairie itself" (Hawker).

When I read that, I thought, *Yes! Hawker found the words to describe what happens when we die—we become sparks beautifully dispersing out into the world.* I also

4

believe that those of us who are left behind can call on those sparks—through the silver strands of light that connect all energy, all life—to come back together as the spirit of that one particular soul we knew and loved. In other words, I believe in angels. I know they exist, even if only because the power of our beating hearts is strong enough to make it so. Cayenne has been my living angel, and she will carry on.

But *right now*, I'm so scared of what it will feel like not to be able to listen to her breath, to open my eyes and see her first thing every morning, to feel her wet nose on my leg, to smell her fur. I will be lost. And I will have to work to find myself again. I know she came here to teach me that I'm never alone, because, truly, with her tangible presence in my life, I never was. She was always with me. She was my home, wherever I went. Now it's time to find out where home is without her. Cayenne was the embodiment of grace—a constant reminder that divinity walked beside me. And now I have to find the grace and divinity within myself.

Adoption Day – July 7, 2005

July 7, 2020

August 28, 2020

Dear Cayenne,

I want to explain what's going to happen today, both for your sake and mine. As much as I can't imagine my life without your physical presence, I've decided that you are ready to leave your body you've known for so long. I want to help you move on to something even more beautiful than either of us can imagine. To do that, you have to go.

So...I'm going to take you out to our "spirit garden," and we'll wander a bit—one of the only things you seem to want to do anymore. Then a person is going to come here and give you something to make you fall asleep. We'll be right there with you, and we will be very sad. This is when we will say goodbye. But understand that it is just goodbye to the way we know you now. Even though I will be scared, you don't need to worry. It's okay that it's hard for me to let go of you. You've stayed longer than you need to for me, and I'm so grateful for all you've given me—confidence, companionship, security, vulnerability, friendship, and true love. Those gifts will always remain. I can hold onto it all, without holding onto you.

After we say goodbye, that person is going to give you another kind of medicine, with an injection in your leg (that you will not feel). This will set you free from your body. Honestly, I can't tell you what will happen in the moments that follow. I do know my heart will break. I may feel very alone all of a sudden. But I promise, sweet angel, I will know that I am not. You and I will be together in new ways, invisible ways. You will run and fly your heart out, faster than you even could here. And you will become part of the beautiful energy of the spirit garden and world beyond. You will always have my love, and I will always have yours.

I will be waiting to see you again soon, my girl…my heart. Go in peace, angel. Go in grace. You have been such a good dog. Such a good soul.

Love,
Mom

Laced with Grace

I haven't had much experience with death. That may be why I feared Cayenne's for years, after a vet diagnosed her with liver failure and gave her six months to live…four years ago. She went on to happily and healthfully enjoy her golden years, her liver having repaired itself. In addition to fear, though, the vet's dire prediction gave me a long time to think about her death. In many ways, that prepared me for it, as did my beloved cattle dog's graceful acceptance of the natural process of growing old and dying.

She died two weeks ago. Her body was done, after sixteen years of living with such boundless zest. In her life, she taught me to feel safe and confident, to be vulnerable and playful, to be patient and listen. I knew her death would also hold valuable lessons.

I had hoped she would choose the time and place, and peacefully fall asleep one last time. I told myself I simply could not make that decision for her. But the first thing I learned from her dying is that I, in fact, could. For one of the first times in my life, I knew something in my gut. She told me, with her body language and eyes, that she was ready to go. She just couldn't will herself to leave her body. I listened, and I trusted.

Ritual and ceremony surrounding love, celebration, change, and death help us to be fully present and to honor those experiences. The ceremony of Cayenne's death began weeks earlier. I walked around our land, specifically a small, wooded area we call the "spirit garden," to carefully choose a spot for her grave, one where I could sit for years to come in silence and natural beauty. She often joined me on these wanderings, and I paid attention to where she liked to be.

I had to start digging—pickaxing actually—before I knew when her time would come; our Texas land is solid limestone in places, and a hole that size would take days of sweaty labor. Sometimes it felt unnerving to prepare her grave before her death…to watch her walk by that hole in the ground where her body would ultimately lie. But I realized that avoiding death, so common in American culture, would not stop it. Instead, taking the time to thoughtfully and actively participate in her transition helped me join her in that state of grace she taught me so much about.

The day the vet was to come, I sat by her bed and read the letter telling her what was going to happen. I created a shrine—photographs, candles, an imprint of her paw in clay—in our living room. I brushed her. I held her water bowl to her mouth for one last drink. When the time was near, we went out to wander that land again. I let her lead the way. When the vet arrived, I cried, even trembled, but I breathed deeply and kept my focus on Cayenne. I watched closely as her body responded to the sedative, her breathing changed, and she collapsed peacefully onto Nathan's lap, where we were sitting side by side in the dirt. I watched the vet shave her leg, place the IV, and then inject the liquid that would stop her heart. I held her as she breathed her last. Her tongue fell out of her mouth, and her eyes went cloudy. I did not turn away.

We lay her on a blanket there under the shade of the cedar trees, bits of sun shining through onto her face. The hours that followed were transformative. With silent understanding, we knew we were right where we wanted to be—sitting in the 100-degree heat with our dead dog. I kept my hands on her for a very long time, smoothing them over every inch of her. I couldn't stop touching her. I breathed in her fur, and her paws that I loved so much. I lay with my head on her chest, no longer moving up and down as I'd watched it do for fifteen years, and I looked at the sky. I was so terribly sad…and yet, totally at peace.

The experience of that time with her transcends words. It was a feeling, a knowing. The kind of knowing we can only experience when we are stripped of distraction, avoidance, and noise. I had never spent time with a dead body. I never thought I would want to. But I now understand how important that was, to hold space for her transition, to take the time to say a long, patient goodbye.

Just as I'd never sat with a dead body, I'd never buried one. I'd sent my other cherished animals to be cremated. But with her, I realized months earlier I could never hand her body off to someone else to handle. I wanted to experience it all, to honor her life by caring for her body in death. Placing the blanket over her, when I could no longer see her, remains in my memory a more heartbreaking moment than her actual death. Maneuvering her body into a plastic cadaver bag was excruciating, certainly not physically graceful. But I thought of the words my friend wrote in a beautiful song, "that our pain is laced with grace."

In her grave, I sprinkled the ashes of the dog I'd loved for thirteen years before her, placed four feathers and three of her favorite toys above her, and covered it all with dirt. We then began carefully placing stones on top, creating a beautiful natural monument. Having been in the heat for hours, we went inside for a short break. When I returned, I found our cat Stoney lying in the dirt next to her grave. Stoney had loved his long-nosed big sister, his protector. He had walked beside her in her final days, as she slowly stumbled around the yard. Now, he lay quietly, very unlike him, and looked at us with unmistakable knowing and sadness in his eyes. He mewed and looked back at the ground. He stayed right there for two hours. Our other cat, Dylan, spent three days of mourning in the corner of the mudroom.

I now sit at her grave every evening (and sometimes Stoney joins me). I light a candle next to her photograph every morning. I feel her all over and around our home and in the sound of the windchimes blowing in the breeze above her grave.

In being fully present, I learned the most important things in this life are those that are not seen, those for which there are no words. I'm a writer. I wrote letters to Cayenne. I had hundreds of "conversations" with her about love and death. I find comfort in putting experiences and feelings to words. But sometimes, I'm reminded that all we really need to know is in the silence. It's in our breath—our first, and last, and the billions in between. My husband and I did not need words while we sat with Cayenne's body. Stoney did not need words to know the moment his friend's soul left her body. I have no words for where that soul is now. And yet, I know.

Rattlesnake

A few days after Cayenne died, I mustered the energy
to resume my regular evening jog. As I ran up Arap-
aho Lane—a steep, quiet, undeveloped street way
back in our neighborhood—a huge rattlesnake shot
up from her coil on the side of the road, hissed, and
rattled. I jumped a few feet sideways, shouted "Holy
hell!" tiptoed backward, then bolted back down the
hill. Adrenaline pumped me the whole way home.

Because they're not uncommon in the Texas Hill
Country, I'd always been on alert for snakes when
walking or running with Cayenne. I was her protector,
after all. But in all those years, we never encountered
a venomous snake, and I'd never witnessed a rattler
actually rattle before. It was rather dramatic.

After I got home and settled down, thoughts of danger and fear dissipated. Instead, I sought out the
significance, the message. In the wake of Cayenne's
death, I'd committed myself to paying attention, to
trusting in synchronicity—that what could just seem
like coincidence, insignificant happenings, or encounters just might actually hold meaning. So I immediately Googled "symbolic meaning of rattlesnake encounter" and emailed my psychic, intuitive friend who
also happens to talk…or should I say listen…to animals.

All sources agreed: *Transformation. Transmutation of dark to light. Rising kundalini (or life force). Healing. Embracing both life and death. Rebirth.*

While the snake represents evil in the Bible, and some cultures consider its appearance an omen, most do not. I personally can't conceive of any living creature, outside of particular humans, as evil, even symbolically. Though I must admit that despite my respect for all animals, the thought of snakes makes my body shiver. Not because I fear their bite or think they are "evil," but just because of how slithery and foreign their movement is to me. Snakes are dangerous, sure. But this rattlesnake—the chief of all snakes, according to the Cherokee—made herself known to me. She was not being sneaky or slithery. I am choosing to believe the animal encounters gifted to me are bestowed by a benign universe.

The snake apparently appears when it's time to repair and replenish your vulnerable heart. Of course there's the metaphorical meaning in the shedding of skin— stepping into a newness, knowing our fresh skin may feel even more vulnerable, more tender when exposed …all part of growing stronger. In learning about the healing wisdom of the snake, I read that we can also use our own cycle of suffering and healing to then empathize with others and do our part to help ease their pain. After we transform, we can support others as they transmute their dark to light.

Learning about the snake spirit and what it might have to teach me has made me see them differently, reminding me of the power of our thoughts and how we choose to use them. I can think snakes are gross, scary, and dangerous, and therefore every one I see will freak me out. Or I can think the snake is an awe-some creature, one that is more grounded, literally, than all others.

There were countless little side roads I could've run down that day. Instead, I ran up the hill. Where nobody else was. Except the snake. I may have been scared in the moment, but that fear quickly turned to gratitude for the reminder that I'm ready to transform into whoever it is that I am without my girl.

And So It Begins…

"Ashley's year of travel." Many adventurers and ramblers would scoff at what I'm calling a year of travel. But I've not gone away from home for more than three days in four years. And when I was gone, I worried about and missed Cayenne—the reason for my homeboundedness. Because I refused to leave her for long, I opted out of a lot of travel opportunities. Last year, I even skipped the beautiful wedding of my beautiful stepsister, sending Nathan up to the Catskill Mountains on his own to celebrate with my family. I also have never allowed myself to spend money on the luxury of non-necessary travel.

So in planning for how I would handle the loss of Cayenne, I decided a while back that when the time came, I would wait a whole year before adopting another dog and give myself the freedom and permission to travel vigorously. She died six months into a pandemic and lockdown…but I'm sticking to my plan. I may not make it to Ireland, but I'm committed to my literal and figurative voyage. This isn't just about getting in a car or plane and going somewhere. It's about pausing to observe, within and without. I feel I owe it to Cayenne to mindfully absorb all she had (and has) to teach me, to slow down and listen to other animals and the natural world, to tune in to my intuition (spirit), to grieve, and to consider what it feels like to be in this world without my companion—to review, with fresh eyes, who I am and where I belong.

To some, traveling as part of the grief process may seem like running away. I think of it more as a running toward—toward perspective and feeling more deeply than possible when surrounded by daily life's distractions, and even toward straight-up fun, all totally possible while also being heartbroken. I consider it an opening up rather than shutting down. So with an open heart and mind, off I go...

"Once a journey is designed, equipped, and put in process, a new factor enters and takes over. A trip, a safari, an exploration, is an entity, different from all other journeys. It has personality, temperament, individuality, uniqueness. A journey is a person in itself; no two are alike. And all plans, safeguards, policing, and coercion are fruitless. We find after years of struggle that we do not take a trip; a trip takes us…Only when this is recognized can the blown-in-the-glass bum relax and go along with it. Only then do the frustrations fall away. In this a journey is like a marriage. The certain way to be wrong is to think you control it. I feel better now, having said this, although only those who have experienced it will understand it."

~ John Steinbeck
My Travels with Charley

See It While You Can

"There are many reasons to ramble 'cross this land
Do not make excuses, see it while you can
North, south, east, and west
Let the four winds blow
Their sweet breath upon your soul"

~ Jimmy LaFave

On the first day on the road on my first trip in my "year of travel," we were driving through northwest Texas on our way to Colorado. It was always a given that that's where I would go first—where Nathan and I had taken Cayenne so many years to celebrate our wedding anniversary. (Nathan has a grown daughter, and I brought Cayenne into our marriage. We made a nice little family of three—and then five when we adopted the cats—and I was happy for Nathan to join me on this inaugural adventure and many to come.) The views along the highway, that I'd grow to become so familiar with during the upcoming year, were nothing but endless fields of dirt, some cows, and every so often a random house surrounded by a few trees looking really out of place in the landscape of nothingness. So I'd closed my eyes, knowing I would not be missing much, and the tears came as they now so often do when I close my eyes.

When I opened them, the road was suddenly lined with tall yellow flowers, as far as the eye could see, bobbing happily in the wind. You might think flowers can't bob *happily*, but I assure you, they did. In that same moment, Jimmy LaFave's "The Great Night" came on the iPod shuffle. My friend Jimmy died a few years ago; his favorite flower was the sunflower. After his death, in a session with an intuitive medium, she advised me to choose an image or symbol that, when it came across my path, would signal that Jimmy's spirit was near. I'd chosen yellow flowers. So...now, seeing all those yellow flowers just as I opened my eyes when his song came on...well, it felt like magic.

I didn't say anything to Nathan about the coincidence (synchronicity?)—I just listened to Jimmy sing this "traveling song" and thought, and felt. I don't usually talk to Nathan, or anyone, about these magical moments. They feel kind of private. Plus, I wondered if I was just being sentimental and making up signs and symbols because I *wanted* to believe. But now, I ask myself, *Who cares if I'm making it up?* Isn't magic ours to make? If we don't believe, it has no chance of being real. And maybe what I'm calling magic is really just a recognition of the unseen divine, of the power of my own soul to manifest healing, growth, and connection. So I choose to believe that Jimmy was indeed wishing me well as I set out to see this land while I can and "let the four winds blow their sweet breath upon my soul."

"I See You, I Hear You, I'm Listening"
Colorado – Part I

Exactly one month after burying Cayenne, we arrived in paradise. I'd joined Airbnb the day after she died. I was a little embarrassed by my lack of Airbnb experience, and I was overwhelmed by options and the potential of misleading photos (I've since become a master, and maybe a little addicted to the site). But after hours and hours of searching and hemming and hawing...I'd booked Casa Buena Vista in Pagosa Springs.

Upon arrival, we discovered the vista was more than buena. We ran around the property like kids on Christmas morning—"Look over here! Oh my god, look at that view! There's a gazebo over there, and a swing on the deck?!" And I noticed there was a nice dog fence around the house, complete with a dog-house. My heart broke a little, thinking, *Cayenne would have loved it here.* She'd joined us on all of our previous trips to Pagosa, but we'd always stayed at my uncle's condo (free), which wasn't exactly dog paradise. I told myself to cheer up and enjoy this new freedom to travel without worrying about her, since the road had gotten too hard for her in those later years. Exercise #132 in the acceptance of her death and learning to trust that she was, in fact, here...hanging around my neck in the locket that carries her photo and a bit of her fur, in the clay paw imprint I'd brought along with us, and in my heart.

On the drive, Nathan had gotten a call from his mom that his much beloved Uncle Bob, who had suffered a massive stroke the night before, would be taking his last breath that afternoon. His children would be meeting at the hospital to "pull the plug." Even with that sad news, we were still euphoric as we breathed in the crisp Colorado air while we settled in among the trees, birds, mountains, and views of not only the rambling San Juan River…not only one pond…but four! We had it all—earth, wind, water, and a fireplace in the kitchen.

Nathan set himself up for a late afternoon writing session out on the lower deck. I made a cup of coffee and sat on the upper deck to simply relax and breathe for a bit. Something I don't often do—just sit—but something I promised to do more of P.C. (Post-Cayenne).

After a couple sips…*bang!* I spilled my coffee, jumped, and yelled, "What the…?!," as a little bird fell right at my feet, gyrated for a moment, and lay dead-still on her back with her long stiff legs pointing skyward. Nathan ran up. We both panicked, trying not to cry. I immediately assured him that the bird was fine. It was just shock. "Let's just give her some time." I went inside to give her space so that when she when revived, she wouldn't be frightened.

About ten minutes later, I saw Nathan crying down at his table on the deck. We looked at each other through the window, then toward the bird. She wasn't waking up. I couldn't help but ponder the inevitability and unpredictability of death—just moments ago this little bird was fluttering around the trees with her friends. Then she flew into a stupid window, and was gone. As we hovered over the bird, Nathan told me that her fate had reminded him to check in with his mom. She let him know that just moments earlier, his Uncle Bob had died.

I picked up the bird. The old me would have shied away from the body. The new me needed to hold her and look at her eyes, her beak, her chest. I studied every millimeter of her beautiful little form. I needed to know the life was gone, so we could proceed appropriately. And, strangely, I was honored by the chance to touch this tiny, delicate dark-eyed junco (we later researched to find out what she was). We don't often get to be that intimate with the body of a bird. She weighed almost nothing. One eye looked normal and alive. The other, not. Her companions were fluttering all about in the pine trees a few yards away. I wondered if they knew. Of course they did.

So, once again, it was time to bury a body. We carefully chose a spot in the yard. We gathered the prettiest stones, and we made a tiny grave resembling a miniature, much less time-consuming version of Cayenne's back home.

I wasn't sad for the bird. It was off now, its energy having sparked out of its body, on to whatever's next. I was sad for the ones she left behind. I was sad for us. Nathan and I agreed: enough death for now. We get it! Everything is born and everything dies. It's not always tragic. His uncle lived ninety-three healthy years, and was then gone in a blink. We weren't sad for his uncle either; he had not suffered. We were sad for the ones he left behind who would never see him smile again, never look in his eyes again.

We know every life is fleeting—ever-so-temporary in the vastness of the universe. We can apply that knowledge to cherish all little lives while they're here—to never take a breath or a birdsong for granted, to be grateful. So many lessons and clichés...so much perspective. For now, I just keep thinking of a line that Craig T. Nelson delivers so masterfully in his role as the patriarch in the series "Parenthood." He and his wife Camille have just started couples counseling. So when she shares a feeling, rather than immediately respond with his own two cents, he calmly tells her, "I see you...I hear you...and I'm listening." That's how I feel about death right now. I see you. I hear you. And I'm listening. Couples counseling can be exhausting, though. All the seeing, hearing, and listening is a lot of work. For now, I'd love just a little time apart from death. I'm sure we'll reconnect again soon.

Traveling Companions
Colorado – Part II

There are few people I would ever consider traveling with. I'm particular. I'm picky. I'm sensitive. I'm an introvert. I'm private in weird ways (i.e. sharing car space, bathrooms, or even kitchens can feel very intimate to me). Nathan is one of those few people—I love traveling with him. For the most part, travel seems to bring out the best in us, as an *us*. Being out in the world, seeing and doing new things, revives a childlike joy and ease that helps us not to take things so seriously, to be playful, to be nice.

But it's not all rainbows and unicorns out on the road. Nathan is a highly sensitive person (that's a real thing—I recommend looking it up if you're not familiar; more on this later). And…he's a writer. For the most part, I've adjusted to what this means for our travel. I know every morning is writing time. We're never going to get up and get to it. Since I sleep about three hours later, anyway, that's often just fine. It does mean, though, I'm always the one preparing the hiking snack, getting things organized and making plans, and tapping my toes once 11 a.m. rolls around and he's still sitting in his PJs with his journal and candle.

I've also adjusted to the reality that 75% of the time we're experiencing something, he's thinking of what he's going to write about it. If I make a comment during a hike or lunch or sunset, I'll likely need to repeat it to give him time to snap out of writer's brain and hear what I'm saying. And yes, I'm a writer, too, but I came to it much later. I'm still developing my writer's brain, so while I do slip into this mode—pondering what nuggets I'll want to tell a story about later and how to best tell it—I'm usually just in regular experiencing and living mode.

The part of our dynamic I haven't adjusted to is how the mood of a highly sensitive writer can go awry real fast. For instance, I just don't understand how you can be in Colorado, with a day of nothing but beauty and outdoorsiness, and find yourself at the end of the day grumpy and depressed. I mean, sure, I get "hangry" all the time. If the drive home from a hike takes a little too long, and I'm tired and have to pee and we've run out of snacks (but, let's be honest, I never run out of snacks because I'm a damn good planner when it comes to the important stuff)…I'm grumpy for a minute. Until I pee and eat. Then I'm back to my lovely self.

When a mood hits Nathan, it's deep and usually irrecoverable until the next day, at least. On this trip, after an awesome hike that went longer than planned and left us both feeling wonderfully exhausted—as in, our legs almost didn't get us back—I was super excited to do some yoga stretches, take a bath, and settle into a late afternoon and evening at our Casa Buena Ainbnb-fantasy-paradise-cabin. I thought we were both on cloud nine. But when I emerged from my bath, I could see it in his face. I know that look. Dejection. *What? How? What happened in those fifteen minutes?* I asked as much.

After asking about ten times over the next hour (perhaps an annoying trait of mine), it came down to: he didn't get to finish his poem that morning, and he'd overworked his body, and was feeling pains in his knee and groin, which of course reminded him of how he ruined his body in his younger years of overdoing it, and now he's falling apart and can't afford a knee replacement, and who would want that kind of surgery during the pandemic anyway, and what if he can't keep doing the things we love to do together. *Phew.*

I at least understand now, after thirteen years of knowing this man, there is nothing to be done, and it's not my fault. I didn't fret about what I might've done wrong to bring on this sudden gloom. I didn't try to make it better. And so, we didn't argue (like we used to in these situations). In lieu of arguing, we opted for silence. As we ate dinner in that silence, what had been cloud nine was now a sad little storm cloud hanging low over the table. I did my own thing after dinner, and we went to bed. It felt lonely, and familiar.

The next day his mood had returned to "normal." I tried to push down feelings of frustration about the one lost night—that insensitive voice saying, "Come on, babe, can't you hold it together for just one week in Colorado?! Give me *one week* of a good mood. Bad knees and all." It's a challenge for any people sharing space, sharing lives, to navigate the state of mind of one another. We should all be free to feel how we feel when we feel it—grumpy, depressed, quiet, low. As I try to allow my husband that freedom, though, I'm having a hard time finding a balance between protecting my own state of mind and maintaining empathy and compassion. When Cayenne was alive, I could always turn to her for a little sunshine if a moodstorm was brewing. (My mom used to sing "You Are My Sunshine" to me each night. "You make me happy when skies are gray... .") Cayenne was my shining energy protector. Anyway, while I try to figure out how to continue to be sensitive with a highly sensitive person, for now, my solution is to forgive, myself and him, and let it be. Really, there is no perfect travel companion, as there is no perfect companion, period (at least in my experience—yay for those of you who have found him or her or them). Plus, we did make some pretty good love that afternoon.

Bear
Colorado – Part III

"If you bring courage to your solitude, you learn that you do not need to be afraid."

~ John O'Donohue

En route to our first hike in Pagosa Springs, nervously making my way up the winding dirt road—laughing with Nathan over what a wimp I am when it comes to mountain roads, and how slowly I must drive to be sure we aren't going to topple over a cliff to avoid hitting a chipmunk—a black bear cub moseyed onto the road right in front of us. I stopped (I didn't have to slam on the breaks because I was going 12 mph), and said simply, "Oh my god." The cub paused, looked directly at us, and warily went back to from where he came, surely back to mama.

"A bear! A baby bear? Are you kidding me? Did we just see a bear?!" Nathan was excited, too, but not like me. He'd encountered bears before. I've always been that person who goes on "guaranteed whale sighting" boat rides the one time there are no whales. Okay, I only ever went on one of those boats when a friend's family took me to Maine, but the injustice stuck with me. I go through life feeling like the twelve-year-old scanning the ocean with utter excitement, waiting and hoping, imagining how wondrous it would be to actually *see* a whale, any wild animal in its wild habitat, but never getting the privilege. Finally, I saw. A cub was just as good as a whale. I got greedy and spent the whole hike looking off in the distance for bears and wolves. (Though I admit, one reason I may so rarely see wildlife is that I typically venture into the wilderness in the middle of the day, having slept through dawn when animals are much more likely to be active.)

Just as I did after seeing the rattlesnake, as soon as I got the chance, I turned to the Googles to learn what this little bear may be calling on me to consider. *A black bear meeting may point to a protective presence in your life. Black bears represent playfulness, adventurous spirit, curiosity, new experiences…learning, growing. Support in times of difficulty. Healing. Reminder of the importance of solitude.*

My fear of being alone had been the most powerful element of my pre-grieving of Cayenne. It's why I know solitude is going to be one of the most important elements of my healing. I appreciate the fact that it was a black bear cub, rather than an adult, who crossed my path. The cub appeared to be alone, but there's no doubt his protector was nearby. He was exploring in solitude, knowing he was safe and supported.

A bear represents strength, bravery, protection, and defending energetic boundaries. Bears are a dominant presence in the wilderness, in tune with earth energy. An encounter may inspire you to consider if you're letting others dominate your energetic space (hm...given my very recent "meditation" on companions, moods, and boundaries, could this be synchronicity at play yet again?). The wilderness—out there and within our own souls—can be scary for those of us who prefer definitive paths, to know exactly where we are and where we're going. Bears don't follow a straight path; they roam freely, as we can also do if we trust our higher self and are able to connect to a primal force.

Bears are all about duality, cycles, and balancing introspection (meditation) with decisive and swift action. I'm not sure I've ever taken decisive and swift action. I'm well practiced with introspection, retrospection, and all other sorts of -spection, so much so that I tend to freeze up when it's time for action. I'd rather just think on it some more, even when that thinking and weighing and not knowing can be anxiety-inducing if not downright painful. This little cub has given me much to be introspective about, and I think I'll keep roaming freely...keep moving without knowing my destination...while I think on it all.

Aspen Applause
Colorado – Part IV

I shot a short video with my phone of the aspen leaves blowing in the wind while on a hike. I sent the video to my friend Betty, and she texted back, "It sounds like they're applauding you!" I hadn't thought of it like that at all. But after her text, I couldn't *not* hear applause whenever those golden leaves rustled.

In planning our trip, I looked forward to seeing the aspens, specifically their changing colors, like someone might look forward to seeing an old lover after years apart. On our first hike, as we approached the first aspen grove and saw all that bright yellow against an impossible blue sky, I was back in my lover's arms. There's just something so unique, so striking—and yet gentle—about them. They really do seem to be communicating when their leaves delicately flutter. Rather than applause, what I'd always heard was something like, "Shhh…Be here now. Shhh…Just listen. Rest. Shhhh."

I rhetorically asked Nathan at one point during the hike, "What if everyone walked through the woods and mountains—particularly the aspens—at least once a week? How much better would the world be? How much more would everyone suddenly know?" When we saw a huge pine tree that had fallen, Nathan remarked what an event its falling must have been.

That led me to ask another rhetorical question: "Isn't it ridiculous…that old philosophical quandary about whether or not a tree makes a sound when it falls if nobody is around to hear it?! What the hell? Like something only exists if a human is there to witness it?" Nathan remarked the squirrel in the tree next to it sure did hear it. Then we kept walking, in silence.

Every so often…well, very often…I touched the locket around my neck and rubbed the little gold circles—one a "C" and one a paw—of my other necklace between my fingers. Sadly, we'd never taken Cayenne on the real hikes with us. In retrospect, I'm not sure why. I think it was because we never became familiar enough with the area to know what we were in for with any given trail and didn't know if she'd be up for rigorous terrain and altitude. When those aspen leaves rustled, they told me she was now right here with me, with them, getting to enjoy it all, to *be* it all. The aspens made me feel like everything was okay. Maybe they were in fact applauding. "Yay, you! You get it now, here with us! You're okay…it's all okay."

These glorious trees are such an obvious reminder of what it means to be grounded, and to soar. Their roots dig deep, connecting them to the source, while they reach for the sky and dance and sway and sing in the wind, in perfect harmony with one another. And when one comes crashing down, the forest remains.

Smiling

Nathan has always wished I smiled more. My whole life, people (usually strangers) have told me to smile. Or if I'm going about my business without a smile, they ask what's wrong. A good friend of mine—one who gets me and has seen me smile plenty, and has also seen me not smile plenty—recently made a t-shirt for me. It's all white and on the back simply states, "Leave me alone. I'm fine." It's true. Most of the time, I'm just fine. Don't ask me to smile to prove it...I'll do it when I damn well please.

Since Cayenne died, I smile even less. It might be the thing I miss the most about her. She never asked for smiles. She didn't care if her antics made me laugh or not. Cayenne didn't need the exterior display of my mouth turning up. And yet, she made me smile more than any human could. Just about every time I saw her, I smiled. First thing when we'd wake up. First thing when I'd walk in the door from running errands. Ten times during any given walk. Smiling was an easy and natural response to her presence.

It's not that people don't make me happy—I laugh with friends quite often. There's just something about observing animals, and interacting with them, that makes me smile, whether the ones I know intimately, or the chipmunk on our hike who was bold enough to jump in my backpack looking for food, or the dog who made eye contact with me in the coffee shop parking lot and wouldn't stop staring at me and wagging his tail, as if he knew how much I missed the company of dogs.

If I'm not careful, now that she's gone, and I don't spend enough time out where the wild things are, I could *easily* go a full day (many, actually) without smiling. Still, as my t-shirt proclaims, I really am fine. Happy, even. I love and am loved. I just don't smile much, and I actually do feel bad for Nathan. I'm sure it's disheartening and frustrating to so often be met with quiet stoicism. I bet it's also something he misses the most about Cayenne—what she took with her when she left us.

Tiny Terlingua
Big Bend – Part I

A month ago, as we hit the road for Colorado, I was *so* excited. Nathan and I took our time on the two days of driving, making it fun, stopping often for snacks and beers or mini-wines or coffee. This time, though, when we hit the road for Terlingua, I felt tired and sad, and anxious about the long drive through West Texas.

Despite my pre-travel teeny-tiny Valium dose the night before (Halloween), I'd been tossing and turning since 4 a.m. Nathan and I had slept in different rooms, which isn't unusual (snoring, etc.), but this time something was stewing behind each of our closed doors. It had to do with the night not going quite as planned. "Things not going as planned" has pretty much been the reason Nathan has a serious aversion to plan-making in the first place. I, on the other hand, love a good plan. But I'm also working on getting better at going with the flow. So I didn't think it was that big a deal when my brother's visit lasted longer than we thought, or when I had to drive him into town to catch an Uber (because he hadn't understood Uber drivers don't typically go out to homes in Wimberley), or when I took the opportunity of being in town to say hello to friends who were enjoying a lovely bon-fire. All of this meant it was a little late when I finally got home for the annual Halloween tradition of watching "It's the Great Pumpkin, Charlie Brown."

Again, I didn't think it was a real big deal. It'd been a fun night with family and friends.

But it had been a big deal to Nathan. He'd closed himself in the guest bedroom and refused to come out to watch the DVD due to the late hour. That, and overdoing it a little on Halloween cocktails, contributed to my awful mood as we set out for Terlingua. The mood was a physical weight, and I just couldn't shake it. I felt none of the adventurous joy of the last trip. Maybe I was nervous that the desert, ghost-towny atmosphere would be a letdown after Colorado, with the evergreens and mountains, a place where my soul knows it belongs. This time, I was headed into the unknown, to places I'd never been.

We didn't say a word on the drive. I slept for most of it, but I perked up upon arriving at the Airbnb, "Tiny Terlingua." Boy, was it tiny. I'd been intrigued to try tiny living for a long time, even if only for eighteen hours. As I unloaded the car and worked to creatively find a place for our un-tiny bags, Nathan was off roaming the property, taking pictures, and setting up his writing space at the outdoor table. My bad mood crept back in. I was irritated. I'd booked this trip alone, made all the plans alone, and now I was settling in alone.

As I've stated a number of times, this utter loneliness was what I feared most about losing Cayenne. I'd been coping with the absence of my soul-dog pretty well for the last two months. But now I was somewhere strange without her. When we went to Colorado, I was able to feel her with me because we'd been there together, to some of the exact spots even, many times. Out in the strange desert, I felt disconnected, untethered.

She had always been the great mood stabilizer—really, mood enhancer—in our home. If I began to cry, she appeared, and I couldn't *not* smile, even through tears. If Nathan began to brood, she nudged her head under his hand, forcing him out of *his* head for a minute. And if we began to get angry, she came in and stood very close to one of us, with her ears slightly down. We immediately had to gather ourselves—how could we be so selfish as to cause this sweet girl to worry?

Our mood stabilizer is gone now. So when I was met with hurt feelings and accusations as I put the first bite of ravioli we'd made in the oh-so-tiny kitchen in my mouth, I lost it. Months of a pandemic and all the stressful side effects had taken a toll on my passionate, empathetic husband. And that toll on him had begun to take a toll on me. I've got a pretty high level of sensitivity myself, and it takes a lot of effort to maintain peace of mind, gratitude, and positivity (perhaps a futile, misguided effort anyway). As I explained after the one "lost" night in Colorado, regularly guarding against his negativity and anxiety (now that we're both home *all the time*) is starting to make me close myself off. I've been distancing myself in order to protect myself. So as he yelled about how hurtful it was that I chose to hang out with friends the night before instead of maintaining our Halloween tradition, I had no patience for it. I yelled right back.

We hurled insults and defenses at one another out in the middle of the spectacular desert under a nearly full moon. Surrounded by nothing but exotic-looking cacti silhouetted against a wildly vast sky, turning from blue-pink-orange to deep blue to black, dotted with billions of little stars, I was struck by how deafening our ridiculous shouts were out there. I felt ashamed and angry at what a waste of time and energy this was. Instead of appreciating the beauty all around us, we just couldn't stop yelling. And there was nowhere to escape. Had we stepped inside the tiny house, I feared we'd fill it up with our toxic bullshit within minutes, poisoning what little air there was to breathe. Instead, we just carved out our own separate corners out there in the cornerless expanse until bedtime. As we crawled up into the tiny loft bed, unable to avoid touching each other like sardines in a can, I said a silent apology to my angel dog for yelling, like I never would have if she were here. And I promised to do better. We're going to both have to learn to stabilize, to enhance, without her.

For some, it might be their human children who "keep them in line," and offer perspective simply with their innocent presence, reminding them how fruitless (and harmful) certain adult human tendencies are—to take things personally, punish others for not meeting our unique expectations, defend our image of who we think we are and how we desperately hope others see us, to yell. For the rest of us, it's animals and nature in general who offer that perspective. When you live side-by-side, breath-by-breath, with an intelligent and sentient being who manages to go through every single day without any of that nonsense—without analyzing and instead just being, without holding grudges and instead just living in the moment—you'd have to be pretty oblivious, or stubborn, or lost, not to follow their example. We seem to be slipping into that oblivion from time to time, without her by our side. But surely…I have to believe…we can find our way out.

Tiny Terlingua

Big
Big Bend – Part II

We woke with sunrise in our tiny house to pack up and head to Big Bend. It was Day of the Dead. While we sat quietly at breakfast, in recovery mode from all our arguing the night before, I checked my phone. Facebook showed me a memory from seven years before: a picture of Cayenne, sprawled out adorably on the carpet as she and I took refuge in my dad's house after our home had flooded (Nathan had been out of town, so it was just the two of us). There she was, on Day of the Dead, looking out from the phone at me with her angel eyes.

Tears dripped down my cheeks as I tried to keep eating my breakfast burrito. Nathan put his hand on my arm. Back in the car he told me he'd try to do better, as if he'd read my thoughts the night before. We began to breathe a little more freely as we stopped at the infamous haunted Terlingua cemetery, and then drove under the big sky into Big Bend National Park, and headed for Santa Elena Canyon along the Ross Maxwell Scenic Drive. We didn't say much, but our breathing continued to become more expansive, more relaxed. Among those big rocks, the big cliffs, the great Rio Grande carving its way between Mexico and Texas, it was impossible not to get some big perspective on our little problems. It was impossible not to think of the centuries it took the river to slowly erode the huge wall of rock towering hundreds of feet above the water. It was also impossible not to think of the big election day looming just twenty-four hours away, when we might finally get rid of the narcissistic nightmare of a "president" who led thousands of people to chant "Build that wall" in hopes of keeping desperate Mexican families out of our precious "Land of the Free." Those are big problems.

All the bigness was humbling. After hiking along the banks, I took my socks and shoes off to wade in that big river, and I felt like a tiny ant moving about in this massive universe. And very little about my life mattered, in the best way. The power of that thought, that perspective, to comfort me helped me remember that the *only* thing we control is our thoughts, and our thoughts determine our perspective. In that way, reality is really ours to make. Unless we let our thoughts control us, in which case we might just miss out on all the beautiful miniscule moments that make up our miraculous lives…because we're too busy thinking and worrying about it all.

Vibes
Big Bend – Part III

Everything has a vibration...every human, every tree, every stone. It's pretty much what this whole universe is: vibes...energy. And I'm not just being a hippie. Even Einstein explained that "everything in life is vibration." String theory proposes that everything we see as matter, as particles, is actually vibration in loops of string, each with its own frequency. It's quite a beautiful thought, if you imagine the pluck of a string on an instrument initiating a vibration that exists forever, and each of us is nothing but a musical note resonating—sometimes in harmony, sometimes in dissonance—with all of the other notes around us.

This exploration of West Texas has me thinking about the unique vibrations of place. I happen to live in a place considered by many to be an energy vortex, with ley lines running through it. Mention "ley lines" to anyone in my hometown of Wimberley, Texas, and they're likely to reply with something like, "Oh yeah, of course." Technically, these are geographical lines that connect significant spiritual or cultural places around the world. But many believe they are more than that. They believe that the lines carry energy, or good vibes. Just as the frequencies of vibrations within our bodies can manifest health or disease, peace or conflict, good moods or bad, it makes sense (to me, at least) that places carry the energy of the people, stories, and events that have existed in them throughout time. And cyclically, the vibes of any place can then manifest within the people and events to come.

Cayenne seemed to have a keen awareness of the vibrational frequency of places. She was generally at ease in most places, but a summer years ago that we spent living in a hundred-year-old farmhouse of a friend was all the "proof" I needed that places carry unique energies. The friend had let us know that a young man had been found murdered in the house a few years prior. Who knows what else happened within those walls over a hundred years. Cayenne sensed enough to bolt out the front door every chance she could—extraordinarily unusual behavior for her. She'd go hide under a parked car, or just lie in the grass. She was okay with the land around the house, just not the house.

I'm not nearly as tuned in as she was, but as we worked our way from the "ghost town" of Terlingua, to Marathon, to Alpine, to Marfa, the difference in the *feeling* of each was undeniable. It's like meeting new people at a party—you usually get a vibe from each one, if you're paying attention. You might sense negativity, or phoniness, or a magnetic warmth that makes you want to be around that person again. Here's my take on the vibes I encountered at this West Texas party...

Terlingua was the seemingly closed-off but poised, confident, and wise woman at the party. When I met her, I didn't dislike her, but I wasn't sure how to strike up conversation. What would we have in common? Quickly, though, I decided she isn't closed-off. She just has no need to impress. No need to engage unless you want to quietly, thoughtfully engage with her. And when you do, you could probably learn a lot.

Alpine was a grumpy, set-in-his-ways old man. The kind that makes you wonder why he even came to the party. I tried to politely ask questions—find out his history and what he was really about—but he gave me and my questions a funny look and made me feel uncomfortable. I wasn't jiving with his frequency.

Marfa was the artist, plain and clear. She cares about beauty. She appreciates good food. Talking to her lifted me up, made me feel good about myself. I didn't go deep with her, so I could be wrong. She might be pretentious or uninterested in others. I'm not making any pronouncements here…only saying what I felt. Anyway, I'd like to spend more time with her. She was fun.

Marathon didn't put on any airs. He didn't dress up. You could tell he doesn't go to a lot of parties but was happy and humbled to be there. No small talk with him. I hate small talk, so I felt at ease with his energy.

My takeaway from this place-energy exploration was that the best way to enjoy a harmonious, albeit brief, relationship with each place was to simply observe, feel, and respect each for its particular frequency. Just as with humans, expectation—or the desire for someone to vibrate at the level we wished they would—is sure to disappoint. The fun of travel is that we're not in a committed relationship. We can move from place to place, just listening to the unique songs each one hums.

Javelina
Big Bend – Part IV

While I was hoping to see a bear or mountain lion on the trip to Big Bend, the animal that appeared to me was the javelina. Not exactly majestic, but who am I to judge? As I put on the brakes to watch a pair of small, black, pig-like creatures trot across the park road to the other side of the desert, I took note. Of course, back at the Airbnb that night, I got online to learn about javelinas. These are courageous animals, despite their small size. They travel in herds, which protects them from predators like coyotes and wild cats. Their wisdom: *Keep in touch, be fierce and tenacious, know there are many paths to your destination.*

I read on. Any kind of boar-related animal can apparently be calling for you to meet an uncomfortable situation head-on. Uncomfortable? Like this heartbreaking trip where Nathan and I just can't seem to find our way to one another? We've tried; we really have. But the sadness hovering around us—the disconnect—is undeniable. As a spirit animal, the javelina encourages us to do this facing head-on in order to finally resolve a situation (a marriage?). Apparently, I'm to believe the result will be a fair and equitable path to peace, once fears are faced. This will lead to personal growth, progress, and contentment.

I'm gonna need a herd of javelinas for this one…

Extended Grief

I could think of nothing else in the days immediately before and after Cayenne's death. I cried all the time. But I kept functioning, which actually surprised me. I'd been preparing so long for this loss, and in all that mental preparing and thinking ahead, I imagined the sorrow might just render me incapable of doing life for a while. My fear had been mostly to do with her actual death and the days that followed—how to say goodbye, how to transition into a world where she would suddenly not be there. As we tend to do, though, I survived. I woke up day after day and went about my business. I thought to myself many times, "Wow, look at me...I didn't think I could do this. But here I am, not just surviving but living. I miss her like crazy, but I'm *okay*."

Five months later, I don't feel okay. I've been struggling with a physical anxiety so severe I lost weight I don't really have to lose (I refer to the anxiety as "physical" because it feels like that's where the origin is; my body—my gut—tells me to be anxious, which then dictates my thoughts about things, so it becomes a battle between body and mind). I'm not one to ever lose interest in food...ever. But I have. I feel fear and doubt when I think of almost all of my relationships— my marriage, my friends, my parents who are dealing with their own sadnesses, even my cats. I feel like I don't know what I'm doing. In a recent text to a friend, I reluctantly used a phrase I hate; I asked her, "midlife crisis?"

For years I've been preaching to Nathan that happiness is a choice—that even in the midst of loss and sadness, every day we can choose to find and feel joy and gratitude. I don't have the energy to make that choice lately. My mind works all day long to solve problems that aren't there. I'm losing the drive to keep working on our marriage and figuring out how to be a good partner, and Nathan is rightfully concerned. In trying to understand, as we sat by the fire a few feet from her grave, he recently asked me, "Do you think all this anxiety has something to do with Cayenne?"

I broke down. Yes. Yes, it does. It hit me: I thought I'd made it through the hardest part of the loss, but I'm actually just now entering it. I have yet to figure out who I am without her. When she was by my side, I always felt confident. I knew what I was doing with her. I knew how to *do* us. I was good at loving her. And she thought I hung the moon. Or so she let me believe. Now I'm adjusting to a world where nobody thinks I hung the moon, a world of human love that is imperfect and conditional.

Despite all the travel and seeking and trying, I'm lost. And if I'm honest with myself, I think I've been hoping and waiting for someone or something else to find me, to save me, to give me purpose...to bring me home. Today, I remind myself that life isn't about having someone else out there who thinks you hung the moon, or someone to save you. I've got to learn that my peace of mind will never come from others, from without—only from within and from the deep knowing that I make and carry my own light.

Mine to Make

In the spirit of making my own light, I planned a little trip to Fredericksburg just for me. A year of travel during a pandemic necessitates lots of small road trips. I may not be flying over oceans to see the wonders of the world, but there's something to be said for the break, the newness, and solitude any travel offers, even if it's a just a cozy casita less than an hour away, in the middle of a pasture of sheep, donkeys, and llamas.

In addition to a bag of comfortable sweats and pajamas, I took with me the framed photo of Cayenne that goes everywhere I go, a few candles, a Christmas coffee mug, and three tiny Christmas decorations. It didn't occur to me an Airbnb rental would be decorated for the holiday. When I walked in to find a lighted tree, I smiled (remember how infrequently that happens now). When I opened the cupboard to find I hadn't needed to bring my own Christmas mug, and a wine glass embossed in gold with the phrase, "Santa's Favorite Helper," I thought I should've booked more time here.

I unpacked my goodies and set up my work space at the dining table, facing the tree, with my candles and photo. I made coffee and a snack, did some work, took a break to walk outside and look at the sheep as they "baa-ed" out back, wondered if I should get in the hot tub yet, went back to my little setup to do some more work, went outside again to get a chiminea fire ready to light after dark, threw out a yoga mat upstairs by the bedroom fireplace, did a quick work-out, went back downstairs, poured a small glass of wine along with a tall glass of sparkling water, soaked in the hot tub at sunset, lit a fire…and on it went.

Every minute was mine to make. This was solitude at its finest. As the sun went down over the pasture with the animals peacefully grazing, I felt myself begin to wiggle free from the long, firm grasp anxiety had on me. Maybe I was starting to get my second wind. Maybe that wind would be enough to re-ignite my little inner pilot light (whenever I'm having a hard time getting a fire going outside, a gust of wind or powerful blow usually does the trick). I think that's been my problem: my pilot light is out. And we all need that small flame to be burning constantly within, so that when we have to spark the big fires—whether to do the hard things, or to love fiercely—we have the gas to do it.

I wonder...

How old do strangers think I am?
Does everyone feel like a kid deep down, no matter
    their age?
What's the line between privacy and lies?
What would my cats change about their lives if
    they could?
Where will I be living in ten years?
Where will Nathan be living in ten years?
Have I hurt people and never known about it?
Who thinks about me? When?
What do they think?
What does it feel like when our bodies shut
    down...when it's time to go? Is it scary?
Did my mom have dreams that never came true?
What will I have for dinner?
When will my next drink be?
Nap or more coffee?
Why do I believe in soul-dogs/cats but not
    soulmates?
How many animals are suffering right now?
Is there one I could help today?
Should I talk to plants more?
How can I learn to hear them?
Why am I most creative when I'm dreaming? Where
    do those stories come from?
What will today be like for the incarcerated man who
    is reading a book I edited in his cell right now?
What do my parents like the least about me?

Why do I pay so much for health insurance that does
　　nothing?
How many babies will be born this year to women
　　who didn't want to have a child?
What will their lives be like?
Do my friends know how grateful I am that they're
　　alive?
Did I know Stoney in another life?
Do I believe in "other" lives?
What would Cayenne's memoir be like?

Gemma

Gemma's eyes are amber glowing fires. She has adorable, floppy ears—golden with streaks of white that match the white patch on her chest. She looks like Benji. She loves peanut butter. And she is the most terrified, grief-stricken dog I ever met.

I.

During my year of travel, I had also vowed to foster a dog. I've always wanted to foster, but Cayenne, the cats, and our animal-human family balance made me reluctant.

I need to pause here for a short public service announcement: Fostering is the only way for us to stop killing dogs and cats needlessly. Only when we all get involved and offer our care and spaces up to animals waiting for homes can shelters save lives through coordination, training, educating, and providing resources. When we count on shelters—typically traumatizing places for animals—to actually house the millions of cats and dogs who've been neglected or who exist because of our irresponsibility in refusing to spay/neuter, they simply cannot keep up, and they kill animals due to space and resource limitations. Not only do we need to stop recklessly adding more, more, more to this planet; we must finally start to care for the life that is here. Fostering is an essential element of putting an end to the suffering and death of countless animals.

In most shelters in most towns, Gemma would've been deemed "unadoptable" and killed when someone dropped her off as a stray. Thank goodness, Austin is a no-kill city, and our local rescue group brought her to Wimberley. I was reminded of my designs on fostering when a friend tagged me in a post about this extremely fearful dog needing a special foster home. I didn't have any trips planned with Christmas coming up…and, you know, the pandemic. I filled out an application immediately.

We'd been told she was "paralyzed with fear," but seeing her in person was a punch to the gut. I'd never seen a dog so shut down. She truly did not move. She didn't register people, except to look away if one approached her, seemingly trying to disappear. Outside in the "play" yard, she sat squished up into a corner of the fence the whole time we were there. We hadn't planned on bringing her home that day—we were just there to meet her. But one minute in, I knew she needed to get into our home—hopefully one still aflutter with the loving energy of Cayenne—immediately. I knew many would be reluctant to bring home a dog from whom they could expect zero interaction, zero play, zero trust…for who knows how long. A volunteer carried her into our back seat, and off we went.

II.

After carrying her inside to what had been Cayenne's bed, where she would spend 95% of her time with us, I began posting updates about her in what I called the "Foster Diaries" on social media. Gemma seemed to strike a chord in many hearts, and I would come to count on the support and kindness of those who followed along on her time with me.

As we entered the holiday season in November—one that lacked the normal happy anticipation due to COVID and family illness along with the hole Cayenne left in our home—I'd been struggling with that "extended" and complex grief. My days were aimless. I'd lost my compass when I lost my girl, and I needed purpose. And while I know I'm not supposed to be seeking purpose from without, fostering Gemma gave me that. After all, we were saving her life…one that I soon came to realize even she wasn't sure she wanted to go on living.

III.

Because Gemma would not willingly move in the presence of humans, lest she be noticed, I carried her out to pee many times a day. She was about forty pounds; my biceps got very sore, and then very strong. Eventually, she did muster the courage to walk from her bed verrrry gingerly out the back door. Getting close enough to her to carry her back in was a time-consuming exercise in patience. I would quietly follow her around and around until she would give up and cower against the fence, and allow me to pick her up. She ate in bed, or at night when we weren't around and she could safely and secretly walk to the kitchen where food had waited for her all day. I'd carry her to different parts of the house to try to encourage her to explore. I'd set her down, surrounded by hot dog pieces that always went ignored, where she would sit looking terrified and uncomfortable. As soon as she felt I wasn't looking, she would creep, with her tail as far between her legs as it would go, back to her bed— her only safe place.

At first, I didn't know her eyes were fireballs. When she came here, they were dark and empty. I consulted a trainer on the phone, and he asked about her attitude, how her spirits seemed. After we talked for a while, we both sadly concluded her will to live was questionable. It was sickening to think of what humans had done to her, but we were encouraged not to, as pity would do her no good. We needed to think positive thoughts on her behalf. Nobody would ever hurt her again, and that's what mattered.

After about a week, she stopped cowering or turning away when we approached her bed, and learned to revel in scratches and delicious snacks brought to her. For the *most* delicious snacks, she'd slowly inch her way along the floor, crawling toward the food and licking it up and then slowly inch back (on her belly) into the safety of her bed. She walked around indoors willingly *only* when we were asleep or gone. If she was forced to walk in our presence (like, if I carried her inside and set her down a few feet from her bed), it was the most silent and slow walk I've seen a dog perform—again, like she was just wishing to be invisible. I hadn't known a dog could tip-toe.

In the beginning she hardly even registered sounds, which I thought odd for a fearful dog. She was just that shut down. Day by day, though, she came to life. She observed with interest, and sometimes she'd startle at the sound of the toaster popping or a gust of wind outside. She was at her best, sadly, when asleep. A week or two in, while we were watching TV, she rolled onto her back while asleep, paws up in the air, head fully upside down. Total relaxation. Nathan and I cried with joy. She was asleep, but in the safety of her dreams, she was happy. From then on, I knew she had it in her. I knew she could learn to want to live.

It took six weeks for her tail to wag. When it did, I cried again. Especially because it wagged in response to me, when I came in to say good morning. The wag was awkward and sloppy, like it was the first time her tail had ever practiced that movement. It was beautiful. I came to love her dirty dog smell (who knows when she last had a bath or if she'd ever). Just as I'd been so soothed by Cayenne's breathing, I loved the sound of Gemma's breathing—her little dream noises and flutters. I loved her Muppet-like paws. I loved witnessing her eyes start to glow. I loved *her*.

IV.

We kept Gemma for seven weeks (a short time, in the scheme of foster-things). Despite the progress of tail wags and a quiet contentedness in our presence, she still never chose to walk inside the house from the yard. Actually, she chose to move less and less when inside, even in the middle of the night. She preferred outside, and it was really hard to get her back in.

Not much about the seven weeks was easy. With the purpose and love Gemma provided me, also came daily questions, failures, and an increase—rather than decrease—in anxiety; I haven't experienced that level of anxiety since the demise of my first marriage sixteen years ago. I would wake up many times in the night, wondering if she was okay at the other end of the house, often going to peek in on her. As soon as I got up each morning, I'd immediately go to work on our routine, as I knew routine was important. After the eating in bed, the going outside, and the lengthy process of encouraging her back in, it would often be noon or 1 p.m. before I sat down to work. By 4 p.m., it'd be time for another two hours or so of indecision and often frustration. If she didn't want to muster the energy or courage to get out of bed to go out before dark, should I keep carrying her out? It was always a question of how much to "make" her do vs. how much to allow her to choose. And the times we inadvertently scared her—by letting the door accidentally close right behind her, or dropping something while she was out of her bed, were just awful. It felt like one step forward, ten steps back.

Friends told me to relax and let go. She was safe, that's all that mattered. She just needed time. I knew all this, but for some reason, she monopolized my thoughts. I was constantly wondering what I should be *doing* to help her. Sometimes, I sat with her and told her about Cayenne and cried. In those moments, she seemed serene, almost soothed by my sadness...perhaps re-

lieved I wasn't asking anything of her. I was just griev-
ing alongside her.

I continued to try not to be sad *for her*. I needed to
exude the confidence and happiness that she could
not experience yet. It was hard, though, to see how
she carried her trauma in her body. Her muscles were
often so tense. In emotional and spiritual work as
humans, so many of us strive to live in the now, to
abolish fear, to heal pain—generally healthy practices.
And we have the gift of words, often making it a little
more possible to process trauma. Words or not,
though, scars and wounds are real and powerful. I
learned from Gemma to have greater empathy for
this, for the reality that it's not always possible or
necessary to fully let go of the past. Gemma's been
given good reason to be afraid, to feel grief. And even
as she learns about happiness, she may always carry
some amount of fear and pain in her body. And that's
okay. That's what she was teaching me: I couldn't
"make her better," and that was okay.

V.

After some visits from a neighbor with her happy-go-
lucky little chihuahua, witnessing Gemma's intrigue
and playfulness with him, I thought she needed to
move on to a home with a dog, someone who could
show her how to be and what to do. After putting the
word out, I was shocked and relieved to immediately
find a family who wanted not just to foster her, but
adopt her, just as she was. I knew it wasn't only time

for her, but for me. I needed to get a hold of my mental/emotional unrest. I might have sought a little too much purpose as a foster mom. I needed to enjoy my break from responsibility, having some freedom to my days, and to learn that freedom doesn't have to mean *lack*.

Still, though, I've never been good at letting go, in any way, with anyone. And so I was in for another lesson, maybe along the lines of realizing love doesn't mean never letting go. We come and go into one another's lives for all sorts of reasons—maybe it's healthiest to simply be grateful for the coming *and* going. Love isn't possession. Gemma wasn't mine. Her trust and her future didn't *belong* to me. I didn't need to worry that without *me* to love her, she somehow wouldn't be as okay as she could be.

So I did it. I let her go, trusting that the universe has her back. I carried her from my car into her bed at her new home, sat with her for a long while to try to comfort her, and sobbed as I said goodbye, and for hours and hours after. I knew it had to happen, but walking away from this girl, who wagged her tail only when she saw me, was one of the hardest things I've done.

Epilogue
Gemma stayed in that home for a couple of months and made progress, but the other dog's energy was too much for her. As time passed, rather than getting used

to each other, Gemma became defensive and even a little aggressive with him. Fortuitously, she went from there to the home of a couple who hadn't been ready to consider her before because they were still mourning the loss of their dog. They thought they were fostering. But they ended up adopting her, and many months later, I received a video of her actually playing with her human, bouncing and barking. It was unbelievably beautiful. Now, when I'm feeling sad or purposeless, all I need to think of is that video. Gemma is not only okay, she's happy. The fact that she got a chance to know play, and to know love…the fact she is home…is everything.

A Complicated Relationship

From the time I was very little all through my teenage years, I *loved* to be alone in my bedroom. It was my personal home within the larger home that I also cherished. I found peace in the safety—door locked, and dresser drawer pulled out in front for extra security—of my solitude, my private space, the easy entertainment of my own company and imagination. I always had plenty of friends, and time with them was equally important to me. In groups, though, friends required energy. And sometimes being among a group made me feel like I was on the outside; it actually made me feel more alone. Going through a typical day at school (and most certainly at parties or dances), I would feel these random waves of isolation and loneliness wash over me, truly for no apparent reason. It would be a relief to just literally be alone at the end of a long day at school. At least then, I was back in that refuge of everything that made me comfortable—without trying to be likeable, or the fear of rejection, or comparing and contrasting myself to others.

Despite my existential loneliness—that I now know most of us feel from time to time—I think a big reason I was able to enjoy actually being alone was that I was lucky enough to have friends and family that I knew were always *there*, right outside my door, or just on the other end of the line. I was loved, and that love wasn't going to up and disappear while I was in my safety cave.

It turns out, whether intentional or not, I spent my thirties designing my life so that solitude is pretty much the default. I gave up classroom teaching long ago. I do all my work from home. I don't "belong" to anything (a gym, a club, a group). I chose not to have children, and I honestly can't fathom the level of not-alone-ness children entail. They are simply *always* there! And I married someone who travels (or did, pre-pandemic) for a living. But through that decade, through all those decisions, Cayenne was here. And I had wonderful friends, near and far, when I craved connection. Then the pandemic hit. Nathan stopped traveling, which meant no more solitude in my home. And sadly, it also meant losing some of those nearer friendships, that it turns out weren't strong enough to withstand the strain of a little social distancing.

And then I lost her—the one I'd been most connected with, in the most pure, effortless way. And now, even though I'm more introverted than ever, I'm often unable to enjoy the recharge that being alone should bring. The feelings of worry, loneliness, and discon-nect are too strong. My mind tricks me into thinking everyone else is out there having a great time, loving and being loved, and laughing. But something keeps me from joining them, even when the opportunities are there. Basically, I'm like a cranky toddler. I want who and what I want when I want them, and then I want them to go away, but remain available to me for the next time I want them. I want to know I'm safe and loved. I want to *be* alone without *feeling* alone.

In her book *This One Wild and Precious Life*, Sarah Wilson helped me to better understand my complicated love-hate, comfort-discomfort relationship with aloneness. She explains that someone with a work-lifestyle like hers, that of a writer, can be extraordinarily isolating, if you let it. Even if you long for company, the transition from quiet aloneness to out-and-about-ness can be jarring. Despite that, or because of it, you must be deliberate about your days, making plans to get out into the world in ways that feel good. Maybe that's the key to falling back in love with being alone—even if it requires proactivity and nudging on my part, I need to intentionally pop out of my safe, but sometimes sad, turtle shell regularly, and then just as intentionally carry the delicate threads that connect us back with me when it's time to retreat again, remembering those threads are always there even when barely visible.

Pain

My therapist once told me, during an extremely difficult time several years ago, "Ashley, I'm afraid there is no way to avoid pain in this situation. No matter what you choose or do. I'm so sorry." As I got up to leave, a total mess, he gave me a genuine, caring hug. He hurt for me.

He was right. I made a choice, and I survived the pain that came with it.

Sometimes I find myself trying too hard to avoid pain...as if there's some just-right way for me to do life, and if I could crack the code, the rest of my days would be pain-free. Then I hear his voice, like it was yesterday: "There is no way to avoid pain...I'm so sorry." And I feel a strange peace. I remember how pointless it is to flail about, trying desperately to dream up ways to escape hurt, which just piles anxiety on top of the pain. I remember that being alive hurts, no matter what you choose or do. I remember that as I take this breath, there are so many people out there who are in such excruciating pain, they may not want to take their next breath. Even in my moments of sharpest pain, I *do* want to take my next breath. For that I am grateful. I want more of this life, to continue to find the grace laced in the pain.

This is one of the attributes I find most admirable about animals. Of course they feel pain—both emotional and physical—just as we do. What they don't do is analyze their pain, or compare it to pleasure, or fear it, or compound it by worrying about what they're supposed to do to stop feeling it. They tolerate it and proceed with life, and if it gets too bad, they call out for help.

None of us can avoid pain. But we can be compassionate with ourselves, and others in pain, simply offering a (literal or figurative) hug and saying (again, sometimes to ourselves), "I'm so sorry," without trying to deny or change it, knowing it will get better. Sometimes, that's all there is, and it is enough.

Rescue

Having a dogless house again, now that Gemma has moved on, has me thinking about yet another complicated relationship: my relationship with rescues, and rescuing. The house feels empty, and it feels strange not to have the responsibility of caring for another as the backbone of my day (the cats require so little). It's both a great sadness, and a relief.

When I found out somebody wanted Gemma, I texted a group of friends. One wrote back what good news that was—that she understood how much I love her (and would miss her), but she also knew how "emotionally overwhelming" the experience had been. My friend was right, obviously, but the rightness of the observation made me feel a little ashamed.

I've always had a tendency to opt for the pets—and people—who are most in need, most hurt or damaged, most sensitive, most "not okay." I want to take them in, heal them, and show them everything is okay now. Even as a very young girl, I wanted to rescue every stuffed animal I could...particularly from those claw-grabby-machine thingies, and the possible fate of being grabbed by some careless kid who would never really love them. My first dog was a terribly sweet, emotionally sensitive little Sheltie, the runt of her litter with a nub for a tail that fell off in the womb. I had an awful time deciding between her—whose beloved

family was giving her away because of "allergies"—
and a beautiful, confident Shiba Inu a fancy breeder
was selling (I was eleven, and so I didn't understand
enough to tell my parents to stick to rescue groups and
shelters in our search). I chose Honeybun, the Sheltie,
because I felt sorry for her, and felt she needed me. In
college, I adopted Asia, a black cat, from the local
shelter because black cats have a harder time finding
homes. I fell in love with Nathan, knowing he'd been
traumatized by past relationships and circumstances
and "needed" to experience real, healthy love (of the
sort only I could provide!). And, of course, Gemma.

Bringing these rescues into my life isn't the
problematic pattern, I don't think. It's what follows…
my desperate need to give them a perfect life and
make them happy and keep them safe all the time, and
the resulting stress. That's where the shame comes in.
Maybe I'm not the strong and sturdy rescuer I thought
I could be. All I want to do is help animals, but then I
succumb to such "emotional overwhelm" in trying to
do everything just right for them. When Gemma just
could not will herself to walk back inside the house
after an hour of trying—on her part and mine—I
sometimes lost my shit (not around her, of course). I'd
go inside and curse and throw things. I'd fall to my
knees crying. Why—after all the trust I thought we
were building, after the fact that she walked inside all
by herself yesterday—would she turn around six feet
from the door and choose to hide in the shrubs, in the
cold dark rain, from me? Of course I wasn't mad at
her (who would blame her?!). It was just exhausting—

all of my over-worrying. I'd often lie awake at night wondering what she was thinking and feeling (such a mystery), what I did right and wrong that day, what I could do the next to make both of our lives easier. I loved having her here so much, but I worried all... the...time.

My best friend Sarah, who is a therapist, recently defined codependency for me: it means you can't be okay until or unless the other is okay. This came up in conversation not because of Gemma, but because of a pattern she was seeing in my relationship to my husband. For years, I've been prone to that same over-worrying, wondering what he was thinking and feeling (such a mystery), what I could do to make both of our lives easier...what I could do make him okay, so that I could finally be okay. I also had to admit to myself this hasn't just been my tendency with him, or with Gemma...the pattern has played out in a number of relationships and friendships. Not only do I want the ones I love to be okay, I want to be the one to make them so.

Damaged, sensitive souls can be particularly beautiful to me; there's a depth there, and often a greater appreciation of love. But sometimes the damage done makes it harder for them to love and trust, making it exhausting to love them. And that exhaustion can cause its own kind of damage on the rescuer...and a damaged rescuer is no good...which has me wondering if it's my turn to be rescued.

Airbnb Wins

Really good coffee mugs.

Skillets that aren't so scratched up that you risk death by toxicity when cooking with them.

Christmas decorations during Christmas.

A nice bottle of wine from a local vineyard waiting for you (Loss: A $4-dollar bottle of André Extra Dry sparkling wine waiting for you).

Eggs from the chickens on the property in a bucket in the fridge.

A bathtub so clean I can get over my fear of soaking in the same tub countless dirty strangers have soaked in. (Super Win: A bathtub with such an amazing view from the window that I can get over my fear of bleachy chemicals used to keep bathrooms in rental homes sparkling clean.)

A fireplace or fire pit. (Super Win: Both.)

A table perfect for writing, i.e. with a view out a window and comfortable chair that hurts neither back nor butt.

Acreage.

Privacy.

Quiet.

Worthy of six stars: Property includes adorable animals, preferably amenable to touching. Friendly cats, miniature horses, tiny goats, alpacas, donkeys, sheep, and horses all qualify.

Palo Duro Canyon

Everything about our trip to Big Bend had been dramatic: Day of the Dead, Election Day, the Rio Grande, massive cliffs, heated arguments. After some relational recovery time, and after Gemma, I was ready to plan another excursion. I landed on Palo Duro Canyon—it may be redundant to say, but in the thick of the pandemic, travel was limited, and I had to get creative about places to go that wouldn't necessitate flying or being around other humans. The benefit of that creativity was learning about amazing places within driving distance. Despite this being *my* "year of travel," I included Nathan on most of my trips. Even with the occasional conflict, we've always loved to travel together, and it's typically more fun to see and do new things with someone who has a contagious enthusiasm for that seeing and doing. Also, practically speaking, hiking isn't the safest activity to do alone, and hiking is what I love to do.

The Airbnb I chose is called "The Hideout." It seemed fitting for the type of week I wanted. I was ready to hide from the emotional drama of fostering and fretting. (It occurs to me maybe I shouldn't share the name of the place, because if too many people know about it, it'll be harder to reserve and harder to hide. But given that I don't think this book is going get Oprah's attention, and that we came to know the owner, who came to be one of Nathan's bigger poetry fans and supporters, I think we're safe.) This hideout is a beautifully done, quaint, roomy cabin with wood floors, walls, and ceiling; a tiny but effective wood-burning stove next to the bed; clawfoot tub and glorious chandelier in the somehow-rustic-and-luxurious bathroom; large screened-in porch; and—the best part—it was all on a property that was home to a tiny horse, Diego the goat, a couple of normal-sized horses, a donkey, and a very friendly black cat.

The eight-hour drive there was long and boring. The surroundings of Palo Duro are dramatic only in their vast nothingness. Just plains. In February, ugly plains of nothing but dirt. And then the second-largest canyon in the continent appears out of nowhere. (Of course, that's the thing about canyons. Their down below-ness, unlike a mountain's majesty on the horizon, makes them like a huge, beautiful secret.)

Our first hike was to The Lighthouse, a "hoodoo" or rock formation with vast views of the canyon. As we sat with our cheese and mustard sandwiches, KIND bars, wine, and beer, we noted the utter silence. No human. No animal. No breeze even. We'd watched some documentaries about the area to prepare for our trip, and everyone talked about the constant, intense wind in the canyon. But this day was still, with a perfectly mild temperature of sixty-five degrees. I soaked up the stillness, the quiet…in the day, and between us. Even the colors of this place were soothing: layers of different shades of pink, yellow, and white rock contrasting a blue sky and the occasional greenery. These colors, this landscape, were apparently the reason Georgia O'Keeffe nearly chose to settle here instead of New Mexico. When she was twenty-nine, she began teaching at what was then West Texas State Normal College (you gotta love that name), and she was inspired, to say the least. Shortly after arriving, she wrote to a friend: "Last night I couldn't sleep till after four in the morning—I had been out to the canyon all afternoon, till late at night. Wonderful color—I wish I could tell you how big—and with the night the colors deeper and darker...I'm so glad I'm out here—I can't tell you how much I like it." We liked it, too.

Each afternoon was a new hike—exploring areas like the Rock Garden and the little winding Prairie Dog Town Fork Red River. (I saw no prairie dogs.) We'd drive the one mile back to "The Hideout," get comfy, and set up at our individual spaces to write and work over coffee. Then, maybe one of the best parts of each day: we'd bundle up for the much colder evening temperatures, make cocktails in the old-fashioned fancy crystal glasses provided, and head out to enjoy sunset with the animals. This family of different-sized equines, goat, and cat were all so chill; they lived harmoniously with one another, and they welcomed newcomers (at least, they welcomed us). Being among them, wandering their territory with them, I was content. And being with them together with Nathan ...well, let's just say a miniature horse might be a slightly more effective, and much more affordable, couples' therapist to consider.

Olive

After the emotional experience of fostering Gemma, I wasn't sure I was ready again, but I'd committed myself to doing this while I could, and when WAG (our local rescue group) contacted me about Olive, I just couldn't say no. They said she'd be super easy. She was a good, happy two-year-old who just needed a quiet place to be for a month while she underwent heartworm treatment.

From the moment she arrived, she attached herself to me and seemed to love me instantly. She really was a good dog. She sat politely every single time a human approached. That was her greeting. A plop. She'd just been spayed, so she was low-key for a day or so. And then it began. As I sat at my desk trying to work, she would come bounding into the office, and pounce me, Tigger-style. She'd literally push me with both front paws, demanding playtime and attention. Her pounces packed quite a punch, as she was about sixty pounds. I was supposed to be keeping her quiet, though, so vigorous play wasn't allowed. Poor girl...we weren't even allowed to go for walks (dogs who've been treated for heartworm need to avoid activities that could raise their heart rate). The people at WAG suggested putting her in her crate for much of the day. She could semi-tolerate that if I was right there next to her, but as the days went on, it became clear she was developing massive separation anxiety in addition to her normal two-year-old energy that she wasn't supposed to expend. It felt like an impossible situation. Because she didn't seem to enjoy being in her crate, we experimented with leaving her out one evening while we left for an hour or two. After all, she was such a good dog. I put gates up to keep her out of the kitchen/dining area and told her we'd be home soon. Pulling back into the driveway, I looked through the blinds, which seemed askew, and said, "Um…Is that Olive standing on the dining table?" Yes. Yes it was. We walked in to find she'd destroyed every single set of blinds on all of the windows. Like a tornado. Wooden shards were everywhere.

Nathan already didn't really like Olive. He felt like she was always giving him the eye, as if to say, *Please go away and leave me alone with my beloved Ashley.* And she had pounced him once quite aggressively while he was lying on the sofa, and maybe nipped him a little in the process. Seeing the blinds all over the house, the utter destruction, I quickly gathered up Olive and put her in her crate, so she wouldn't witness our anger (I was really upset, too, in addition to being scared of how upset Nathan would be). Crying, I called the WAG foster coordinator. She said they would, of course, pay for the blinds to be replaced, and again, advised me to just keep her in her crate. So that's what we did from then on if we left and sometimes while home, and she proceeded to destroy about five "indestructible" beds/mats in her crate before I gave up, and she had to sleep on the plastic tray bottom.

When I walked around the property with her on a leash (she couldn't go outside without a leash, lest she frolic or run), or when I sat close to her, or when we took her to a friend's house, she was lovely. She listened. She sat and lay down on command. She didn't try to get on furniture. She was great. She just could not be alone, at all.

Thank goodness, Olive was adopted by a friend of a friend just days before I was set to leave on my big trip to Utah. I later learned that after months of experiencing her separation and storm anxiety, they decided to put her on medication, and that along with all the exercise she needs and was now allowed, seemed to do wonders. She's living a happy life with them. Just like with Gemma, when she left, I promised her I'd love her the rest of her life. I asked her to remember that if she ever felt sad or scared—that there's someone out there who will always love her. Those promises have been incredibly easy to keep. For as short a time as I knew these two very different girls, they took their places in my heart on day one.

Many of my animal-loving friends tell me they could never foster, because of the letting go involved. As someone who is *terrible* at letting go, I get it. It's not only that we have to let go, it's knowing the animal—who inevitably gets attached—also has to. Understanding that fostering is so essential, though, to save lives, I choose to view it as an opportunity for more love. Olive and Gemma both have my love forever. I have theirs. Sure, I miss them, and the goodbyes were beyond difficult, but I can't imagine never having known them, and had they not been fostered, they would have been killed. It's really a no-brainer, a no-hearter.

Solo
Best Friends – Part I

The apex of my year of travel was to be the big solo trip to the place I've dreamed of visiting for my entire adult life. Not only would I be flying for the first time during COVID, but this would also be my first time going on such an adventure totally alone—not meeting anyone there, not knowing a soul along the way.

I poured countless hours into planning this pilgrimage to Best Friends Animal Sanctuary in Kanab, Utah. To get there, I'd be flying from Austin to Dallas to Phoenix to Page, Arizona. I knew nothing about Page, except that it had a small airport as close as you could get to Kanab. As I dabbled online, I realized it would be worth spending three days there, enjoying a cool Airbnb and poking around the natural wonders in the area.

With all the flights, airports, rental car, and four different lodging situations, I knew something would go wrong somewhere along the way. In voicing that fear to my best friend, she reassured me that I could handle whatever came up. How bad could any problem be? Right. That was, after all, a big part of my motivation to travel alone: to handle stuff, all by myself, with grace. To be a big girl. So I would take things as they came, be present, remain calm at all times, and trust.

I broke my vow three hours into the week.

My first plane took off late. I knew I'd have to run through the Dallas airport—escalators, trams, moving sidewalks, stairs up, stairs down—to get to my next flight. But I was optimistic. It was the same airline, after all, and the lateness was their fault. Surely they would let me on, as long as I made it to the gate by departure time. After all of my awkward jogging, carry-on bag in tow and mask on my face, I arrived at a desolate gate. The very stoic flight-boarder-lady, not registering in the slightest my frazzled state, or my admirable efforts to make it in time, calmly said boarding was over. I argued, "But I see the plane. It's right there!" No. The plane needed to take off on time (like the one I just got off of...of the same air-line...that did *not* need to take off on time, despite perfect weather and no explanation of any problems?). I thought surely I'd just talk her into letting me on. Unlike the large, overbearing man who'd arrived just as I did, heaving and yelling in disgust, I was being quiet and kind. Tears welled up in my eyes. "Can you please just let me get on? I've made so many plans. If I miss this flight, there's no way to get where I'm going."

No go.

As my mind ran over the domino effect this would trigger, I began crying uncontrollably. I doubled over in physical pain. The lady asked for my name, and typed for a solid two minutes—I'm not kidding. 120 seconds of furious typing. I thought, *Okay, she's really going to work on a solution for me, with all this typing.* She was typing so long, I called Nathan so he could also begin trouble-shooting for me. Finally, she stopped and asked for my name again. *What?* Apparently she'd been typing and typing about some unrelated matter. She wasn't even trying to help! *Doesn't she know my whole trip is falling apart before her very unalarmed eyes?!* This time, she feigned working on my situation by striking two computer keys and reported with zero emotion: "There is nothing until tomorrow. You'll need to go see the service desk."

As I jogged toward the service desk (of course having no idea where it actually was), I called Nathan again. I was a pitiful sobbing child. No calm. No grace. Just utter panic. I couldn't fathom a solution. Either I give up on the whole damn trip—blow well over a thousand dollars—and rent a car so I could drive home from Dallas, tail between my legs...or? Or what? What else? I couldn't spend the night in Dallas. Where would I stay? Where would I eat? (Where and what I would eat is always foremost in my mind...and the possibility that food might not be available to me at any given time is reason enough to panic.)

I couldn't keep running and talking, so I hung up and managed to find the "service" desk...where there was not a soul to provide said service. So for a third time, I called Nathan, still crying.

"I feel like I'm gonna throw up. What can I do? My Airbnb…my rental car reservation at the airport in Page…it's all totally messed up. I just want to come home. I just want to come home. Everything is fucked up." My only excuse for totally falling apart, besides how important the destination was to me, is that all emotions had been heightened by the pandemic and lockdown. Hotels and restaurants weren't options to me. This was my first attempt to return to the great big scary world, and it was as if the world was telling me to stop trying.

When a human finally showed up at the counter, now with about 100 people in line behind me—all in a similar situation but none, as far as I could tell, cry-ing—she seemed to be, albeit stoically, sympathetic. She put me on a flight to Flagstaff, *seven* hours later, and said I could, of course, rent a car from there to get to Page.

I found a place to sit—not far enough from unmasked humans—to have a beer while I got out all my printed-out travel plans and went to work on re-doing the puzzle. I sent a group text to Mom, Dad, and my brother. Seriously, someone might as well have died the way I was acting. *I need you all now. Parker, you're good at Uber. Tell me about it. Dad, you're good at being strong and solving problems. Make me feel better. Mom, you're good at wallowing with me. Reassure me that I'm not overreacting.*

In the seven hours I had to kill, I learned that I could not, in fact, rent a car from the Flagstaff airport, or anywhere in Flagstaff at all, because the rental places all closed at 5 p.m. After an inordinate amount of texting with my family, my dad ended up arranging for a private driver to take me to Page…literally the only option to get from one relatively small town to another very small town at 10 p.m. It would cost $400.

Hours later, while stuck on the tarmac (one of my worst nightmares) on the once-again-delayed flight to Flagstaff, now dark outside, I got out my journal. I wrote in the dark because not a single person had their light on to read a book and I felt guilty about turning mine on. This is what I wrote:

Losing my mind.
No control.
So many humans so close to me. Trapped.
I want to run home.
I want to get away from these people.
I will NEVER fly again.
Bye-bye grace.
I hate this. I hate this.
I want to quit.
So unfair! All this money on flights and a nice place to stay. For what?!
Is American gonna pay me back?
Thank you, Nathan, for stepping up. You're better when you're not in it.

I want Stoney. I want Cayenne.
Cayenne, are you here? Help. I'm trying to trust.
Thank god for vodka...

I cried one last time when the plane took off after sitting on the tarmac for an hour. This time I was crying out of sheer exhaustion and relief that I was, finally...*moving*. It turns out I have a long road—many long roads, with lots of turns, and no map, because that's the whole point...there is no map—to find grace in the face of what I cannot control.

The Rental Car
Best Friends – Part II

My obsession with control became most clear when I turned the ignition of my bright blue little rental car, there in the tiniest parking lot of the tiniest airport I'd ever seen.

I'd arrived at the Page Airbnb at 1 a.m. the night before. The $400-private driver found me at the Flagstaff airport (also tiny, but not as tiny as Page's), said he needed to use the restroom where he remained for seven minutes, and we were off. He was friendly, but I was beyond exhausted, so I was relieved that he was semi-distracted during the drive with multiple phone calls from his wife back home. While trying unsuccessfully to rest (I was just too anxious for this all to be over), I did comment to him how in-the-middle-of-nowhere we seemed. No streetlights, or signs, or anything. Just utter darkness. He explained that's why he was my only option. I barely remember arriving at the house. I'd texted the hosts earlier in the day asking what one might do to find some dinner after midnight in Page, with no car. They ever so kindly offered to leave an Amy's frozen veggie lasagna dinner for me. I microwaved it, scarfed it down, and passed out.

After checking the place out the next morning, now that I was coherent, and happily discovering a lovely backyard where I couldn't wait to relax, I called a cab (something I hadn't done in I can't remember how long) to drive me to the airport, where I had to wait about thirty minutes for the Avis employee to show up to what was literally an empty building, except for myself. I'd never seen an airport without a human in it. Then...finally...sitting in that driver's seat of the bright blue Kia Soul, twenty hours of tension carried in my gut and shoulders immediately dissipated. No more airports and agents telling me what I can and can't do. No more being held captive in a metal tube on a dark tarmac surrounded by germy strangers, going nowhere. I was free.

Despite having to get back home, and my plans for Montana in a few months, I'd sworn off flying (the ultimate sacrifice of control) just nineteen hours earlier. Sarah Wilson, whom I referred to earlier— she's a lovely writer and traveler (who has struggled with beyond-severe anxiety most of her life)—describes our "edge" as that place beyond where we've been comfortably "plonked." The utter relief in simply being able to control my own movement made me realize what my edge, where I'm called upon to be curious and courageous (and so often fail) was: putting my physical form in the hands of someone else. I think I can deal with plans gone awry just fine—as evidenced by A) a year-plus of a pandemic-shaped world and B) my recent eight-hour roundtrip and $150 Airbnb just for a COVID vaccine I didn't end up getting...which I was able to laugh off. I didn't mind the waste of time and money; I was still steering my own ship. It's when there is not a single thing I can do, not

94

an ounce of control I can claim, when someone else is steering my ship, that I come close to teetering off my edge.

It was once recommended to me that I start my mornings off by saying the following: "I trust that the universe will put me in the right places with the right people throughout the day in order for the highest good." This type of mantra is one way I'm supposed to find that courage and curiosity when I meet my edge. It sounds great…but does trusting the universe have to include trusting American Airlines? Can I be courageous and curious from behind the wheel of my little blue car? It's a lot to ask to believe that stuck on a plane on a tarmac is ever the right place for anyone to be, in order for the highest good. And there is a fine line between this mantra and the old standby, "Everything happens for a reason," which I don't really believe. I mean, sure, there's a practical reason for a plane not to take off on time (sometimes), but that doesn't mean it's some divinely orchestrated event. The mantra, for me, is more about the attitude and spirit that we bring to all we can't control. After all, I wonder…What might have happened differently (and perhaps for the worse) had things gone "smoothly" and as planned—had I been able to control things every step of the way? Maybe some other chain of events, far less desirable, would have been set in motion. You never know. So I can get behind choosing to believe that nobody is out to get me and that it'll serve me better in the long run to chill out when I have to relinquish some control. I seem to remember very recently writing about the fact that all we can really control, anyway, is our thoughts. Which goes back to the mantra: "I trust that…"

Be Still

"Be still and know that I am God."

I don't go around quoting the Bible much. But I do keep this one on a magnet on my fridge. It's sort of like those Aspen trees telling me to just be quiet…and know. It makes so much sense that in order to know *Spirit*, to know ourselves, to know love, to be wise— that we must be still and be silent from time to time (like, a lot of the time). Otherwise, we're not really paying attention to all those things that are hard to see with the naked eye, hard to hear with the naked ear…all the magic, all the synchronicity. Yes, it makes so much sense, and yet, I rebel against stillness every chance I get. I have to laugh at myself; it's like I've been handed the key to enlightenment, and it's so easy to just put it in the lock and turn, but I won't. I won't stop moving. My proclivity for motion vs. stillness is evident in so many areas of life: I prefer HIIT (high-intensity interval training) workouts and almost always skip Shavasana (corpse pose) when I do yoga; when I go to the beach, I swim in the ocean instead of lying in the sand; I prefer to clean the house while watching a movie at night, rather than just sitting on the sofa; I love to run and almost never stretch before or after.

I claim to want to know "God"—and therefore to find home—and I know that requires being still. So

what am I running from, I wonder? It can only be that
I'm afraid: what if I'm still…and I still don't *know.*

Near Lake Powell

Lost
Best Friends – Part III

"Getting lost is not just about losing your way. It is about losing yourself…in new experiences, and about learning more about yourself. Travel presents us with a chance to break out of our familiar routine and challenges [us] in a way which would be impossible back home. It's a source for growth and strength and we should happily welcome it."

~ *Phillip Dukatz (travel blogger)*

On this trip through Arizona to the Sanctuary in Utah, I experienced a lot of momentary lostness, and I didn't like it. I realized how quickly I get all panicky—either freezing or fleeing ("fight mode" really isn't my nature)—when I think I might be lost. But as I think back on all the times I felt lost, driving unknown-to-me streets in unknown-to-me towns, or hiking unknown-to-me trails with no map or phone signal— one thing that strikes me is that I was never, actually, lost. There's a big difference between *feeling* lost and *being* lost. We can feel lost any time we're not exactly sure how to get back to our starting point, to safety; any time we're not exactly sure if a relationship should continue; any time we're not exactly sure what we believe about ourselves, or others, or what we're doing with our lives. Actually *being* lost, though, implies we are no longer known (to others or ourselves)—that we can't begin to perceive of a way out, a way home.

In the Dutch tradition of "dropping," parents provide their children with the *opportunity* to feel lost. Pre-teens are left in the woods at night to find their own way out. The adults may be monitoring, but they never help. The culture seems to embrace the symbolism and significance of the dropping event. Kids need to learn what to do to find their way when nobody will help them, to cope with lostness (which I think is just, if not more, important than learning how to actually use a compass or whatever other outdoorsy skills). The skill is learning not to panic, but to trust that there is obviously a way, and with calmness, any one of us can find it.

I was never "dropped," and I've never bothered to learn any skills to find my way out of being lost, physically, or how to remain calm. I thought I had some tools for navigating spiritual and emotional lostness, though this year is showing me they could use some sharpening. This lack of experience and know-how seems to come back around to how much I've always counted on others. When I hike with Nathan or friends, I pay little to no attention to where we're coming from or to landmarks because I assume they'll know the way back. And if not, the chances of two people figuring it out always feel pretty high. When you're alone, you have to pay attention.

Because I'm a safety-conscious kind of girl, I wasn't about to go off on long, challenging hikes with poorly marked trails alone, intentionally at least. On my first day in Page, I drove a few miles to the Hanging Gardens walk. To call it a trail would be a misnomer. It's an easy one-mile walk to a not-very-impressive destination you can see ahead of you for most of the walk. The path is lined neatly with stones. My Airbnb host, though, had told me I could make this a more substantial hike if I meandered away from the trail toward Lake Powell. My ten-minute walk to and from the tiny bits of greenery growing among the rock just wasn't gonna cut it for my day's adventure. So I took his advice.

I veered off-trail and began to pay attention. Every few minutes, I stopped and did a 360. I noted exactly where I came from and the position of the sun in the sky. I wasn't too worried since I was walking toward a huge lake. To get back, I would just need to walk away from the huge lake. Every now and then, though, I would descend from a small hill in this other-worldly landscape made of white rock and red sand and suddenly turn around and not be able to see where I came from. Each time, though I knew I was mere steps from where I *could* see, my stomach did a little flip. My mouth got a little dry. My heart beat a little faster. Every time, I laughed at myself. *Geez, you are such a wimp.*

I made it to the lake and enjoyed the expansive views of dark blue cutting through the canyon rock with the occasional boater zooming silently by, too far away to hear. I guzzled some water. It was cool, temperature-wise, but the Arizona sun—with not a tree to be found—was intense. I'd moseyed around to get some pictures, so when I turned to head back, I felt it again...stomach flip, mouth dry, heartbeat speedy. Technically, I knew I couldn't actually be lost. But a little voice kept trying to convince me how easy it would be to break an ankle, rendering me immobile only to shrivel away unnoticed under the pounding sun.

And so I rushed, trying to outrun the feeling of being lost, which just made me tired and thirsty. I just couldn't keep that physical-emotional response at bay despite all logic. I paused for a swig of water, laughing again at how silly my fear was. As I caught my breath, I saw something move up ahead. This was a very bleak landscape. The only sign of life I'd seen were the footprints of one tiny bird in the sand. But now, out of nowhere, a white fox was dancing in front me. *White*. When he stopped moving, he blended right into the rock. He bounded quickly and easily over the layers and mounds. Then he stopped and stared down at me from above before disappearing.

Now relaxed, I rubbed the locket hanging over my heart—carrying Cayenne's picture—between my thumb and forefinger, and I thanked her. No longer afraid, no longer alone, I reminded myself to stop being so serious, and I pranced off, if one can prance slowly and calmly, in the direction of the fox.

After these experiences of feeling lost and ending up okay—more than okay, I realized how much I would have missed out on the little surprises, the beautiful adventures, the lake views, the fox had I not been willing to get just a little bit lost. It's amazing what we can find if we learn to quiet the fear and instead get curious. Fear is of no use, but if we can avoid that temptation to flee, we can pause, listen, look, and learn (stillness and being vs. freezing as a survival response). Being lost gives us a chance to ask questions, sometimes silently of ourselves, and to seek guidance from kind strangers, Airbnb hosts and foxes included, who may know something we do not. It gives us the opportunity to more closely connect with place, with others, with nature, and ourselves.

I'm borderline addicted to familiarity in my life, in my spaces, in my relationships, in my routines (even in my dogs)...but I know I need to dare to walk into the unknown from time to time, to get lost, and to see what unimaginable adventures and surprises await. We have to be willing to stray from the familiar, ask questions, and seek guidance in order to learn to find our way, whether that be back home or forward to some new home we've never known.

Fox
Best Friends – Part IV

Gray foxes are common in the Texas Hill Country, so I see them crossing the road from time to time, usually in pairs. But the white fox (research suggests it was a kit fox) in the rocky landscape off the shores of Lake Powell…that was a unique encounter, to say the least. Kit foxes are particularly elusive, and while they do make their homes in dens in the desert, it's unusual for one to romp about on her own in the midday sun. They're shy animals and almost totally nocturnal, "rarely seen by humans" according to the National Park Service. In other words, this sighting was to be taken seriously.

Native American wisdom perceives the fox as a helper, especially for motivated and active people. In Celtic culture, the fox symbolizes intelligence. Foxes are known to exhibit quiet observation and calculated risk-taking. They're creatively intelligent and flexible; they can do whatever they put their minds to. They embody a connection to intuition—a clear knowing. The fox may appear to encourage us to nurture these gifts within ourselves, and to remind us to trust our inner voice. Sooo…basically the fox embodies all that I hope to learn to be, all that this year is about: learning to be "frisky" and creative but also be quiet, to not only trust my inner voice but to begin by learning to *hear* it—sometimes it can be very weak, just a whisper, afraid to speak up.

Fox Spirit also represents an awareness of energetic boundaries. As their beautiful and protective coats denote—they show themselves to us to remind us of our own invisible layer of protection: our energetic field. They help us tune in to where our energy ends and another's begins. I'm in desperate need of that attunement. So often, when we're empathic and loving, the energy of those we love—or even just those we know—can overpower ours. I've become well aware of the lack of energetic boundaries between me and Nathan. And I fear what will happen if I don't find a way to healthfully put those boundaries in place.

Physically, foxes are so agile in their movement. Watching that kit fox, it was like she was one with the landscape. They can encourage us to be aware of our surroundings and think on our feet—to *gracefully* adjust to quickly changing circumstances. When we're in alignment with Spirit, we're able to trust our ability to navigate our own literal or figurative landscape.

Cathedral Wash
Best Friends – Part V

Risk-taking, putting myself in any kind of danger, is not for me. It's not how I get my highs. In fact, I was so determined to avoid risk that when the kayak company called the day before my scheduled four-hour excursion to offer me an out due to windiness and "possible excitement," I accepted their offer gladly. The guy was very nice and had noticed I was going to be solo, which was why he gently recommended I may want to stay out of the water that day. He suggested the Cathedral Wash hike at Lee's Ferry instead, as a safe and laid-back way to get outside and see something new.

I arrived at the trailhead for the piddly three-mile roundtrip where a few other cars were parked. It gave me some sense of security to know other humans would be on the hike. (Except for that really sad twinge of fear I get every time a man walks by me when nobody else is around—sad for men that this fear has been instilled in me, sad for women that it exists for a reason. I actually had to explain to myself at one point, after passing two guys and feeling a bit nervous, that it's highly unlikely anyone goes off on a hike and decides instead, "Oh, hm, we could easily assault that woman real quick right here in this canyon. Let's do that instead of the hike!") Anyway...

I read the sign at the trailhead that assured me this hike was for any level of hiker, as long as you pay attention to where you're putting your feet. (On the way back, I took a photo of the actual wording of the sign, realizing maybe I should've taken it a bit more seriously: "This *adventure* has no major technical challenges, but *scrambling* and careful decision-making are needed to choose safe routes over *ledges and drop-offs*." Next time I come across a sign that refers to "scrambling," I think I'll pass.) I texted Nathan to let him know exactly what trail I was about to embark upon and that he should hear from me in two hours.

Ten minutes in, the hike got very slot canyon-esque. The part that was amenable to passing through was narrow, with canyon walls on either side. Then I got to what first appeared to be a large puddle but upon closer inspection seemed to be an infinitely deep, ten-foot-long spring. The trail disappeared into this spring with almost totally vertical canyon walls on either side. *Hm.* Before reaching it, I'd seen a solo hiker—a young man—bounce with ease from side to side of the canyon over the pond...left, right, left, done! My knees don't do that. My bounce isn't that wide. I swear I stood at that puddle/pond/spring for at least twenty minutes. I'd awkwardly hug one side of the canyon wall, seeing if I could affix my foot anywhere, then back away. Try again. Repeat. I kind of wish some video footage existed for entertainment's sake.

I kept trying one side, then the other. I considered the bouncing. Each time I put my foot on that steep slope, daring to take the first step, my stomach sank and I just knew I'd end up in the water, and if I fell in, it'd be a full-body experience. Clothes soaked, phone possibly ruined, etc. I thought seriously about turning around. Somehow though, finally, I scrambled by (the sign was accurate!), clinging with hands and feet to the vertical rock. *Phew.* Surely that was the end of it. Easy going from here...

Nope. The scenario repeated five to six times. I would just stop and stare at what was ahead, thinking, *How? My body can't do that! And if I make it up—or down—that terribly steep rock wall there, can I then make it back down— or up—on the way back? Can I jump up five feet after I've jumped down five feet?* Every time, I considered turning back. And every time, I felt true, visceral, bodily fear. I had no interest in a broken bone.

But I'd seen all types of people returning from the destination—the Colorado River—and they didn't seem scared. They were casually chatting and laughing amongst themselves, some more athletic looking than others. At one point, I struck up a quick conversation with a young woman in a group, seeking comfort and commiseration. I asked about what was ahead, saying I'd come across a few spots I barely made it past. She said, "If I can do it, you can do it." I repeated that to myself for the next hour, over and over.

I did make it to the river. Normally, that's where I'd sit down on a rock, get out some cheese and a beer,

and savor a reward at the halfway point before heading back. I couldn't this time...I wouldn't enjoy it. I
was too scared about the return. I needed to know I
had made it, without broken bones, before I could
relax with a beer. And honestly, I wasn't sure I could
handle the physical challenge even with just one beer
in me.

Shortly into my return, I passed a couple. The woman
was the only other person who was clearly as nerve-
racked as I was. She asked me if there were any more
scary parts. I reassured her. As we yelled at each other
across the canyon, they advised me of what they
thought was the best route where I currently was (it
was not apparent as I stared ahead at my options). It
was like some twisty-turny puzzle of rock and slot that
made it impossible to determine where you came from
(left wall or right wall? up or down?) or what would
get you through the next tenth of a mile. If you started
to walk on one ledge/side, you could easily reach a
point where you simply couldn't go any farther without leaping twenty or thirty feet down.

In the end, it just took patience—knowing there was
most certainly a way, and trusting that my body could
navigate that way without breaking itself. By the time
I emerged from the canyon, my leg muscles were jello.
I got in the little blue rental car, cracked open a beer,
and chugged.

Cathedral Wash will forever be associated in my mind with fear of physical injury. And pride. I did it. I powered through the fear and didn't give up, so I could make it to the mighty river. Two days after I got back home from this trip—seven days after the hike— I woke up in the middle of the night inexplicably and severely nauseated and feverish. I took Pepto Bismol, moaned for a couple hours, and returned to sleep, feeling fatigued the next day, as if I'd been vomiting all night. I believe that was my body processing the leftover fear. I felt physically wonderful the entire week of the trip...never even a tiny stomachache, which is odd for me given my tendency toward irritable bowels. My body clearly held itself together, gifting me with its perseverance so I could have all of these amazing experiences and take it all in. But my fragile little system had to go through some recovery in the aftermath. As athletic and strong as this tomboy has always liked to fancy herself, it turns out my in-stinctual desire to protect this precious body far out-weighs any need to seek an adrenaline rush. Again, it's not how I choose to "get high." All I need for that is vodka.

Arrival
Best Friends – Part VI

As I turned off Highway 89 from Kanab into Best Friends Animal Sanctuary, tears surprised me by not only welling up but continuing to roll down my cheeks, one after another. This was not the panic-based sobbing from days earlier when I missed my flight and thought all my plans were going to hell. The tears were because I was finally here...and it turns out here was a home I'd never known I had.

About fifteen years ago, I decided Best Friends was *the* model of an animal sanctuary, "sanctuary" being the key word—not just a shelter, not just a rescue organization...a sanctuary. When I learned it was an actual destination—a place you could stay, volunteer, *be*—I added it to a very short list of places I must travel in my lifetime. As an organization, they do wonders for animal welfare nationwide as they are leading the charge for us to become a No-Kill country by 2025 (meaning animals are not killed in "shelters"). As a sanctuary, the 3,000 acres were designed not just to rescue and move animals somewhere else. It's a place where animals nearly everyone else would've given up on can actually live forever in peace and comfort. It's a place where the spirits of loved animals hover in every molecule of air and sand.

There are only twelve cabins and cottages on the actual property. I hadn't registered what that meant in terms of quiet and solitude. Immediately after setting my things in my modest cabin—perfect in my eyes, I drove the road through the property. I'm not sure I've ever driven a happier four miles...past Horse Haven, then Angel's Rest, up to Gratitude Garden, by Wild Friends, Bunny House, Parrot Garden and Cat World, and finally Dogtown. On the way back, I pulled into Gratitude Garden and Angel's Overlook, having no idea what I would find. I got out of my car and was met with the sound of hundreds, maybe thousands, of wind chimes singing in the trees.

Row after row of octagonal stones mark the places where ashes of beloved animals have been buried. Every *single* one had personal tokens on top. Every one had letters etched on it that spelled out the animal's name. Every windchime also carried a personal message, epitaph, or photograph in honor of a loved and lost animal. And they sang and sang and sang. And I cried and cried and cried.

Of course, I was thinking of Cayenne. And I felt closer to her than I had in many ways since she died eight months earlier. But it was more than that. I was blanketed in the soul-knowledge that I was surrounded by, covered in, angels. Angels of the best sort. (Yeah... I'm rating angels.) Every chime was a symbol of love shared between human and animal. Every grain of soft red sand under my feet felt holy.

After settling in back at my cabin, which was clean but carried the smell of dog, making it that much more homey for me, I packed up a cocktail and snack and returned to Angel's Overlook for sunset. Sitting on a massive rock, looking out at the impossible pinks and oranges, I believed I was in actual heaven. I was a kid who'd met her celebrity crush only to find they were even better in person and, even more, we were going to be best friends.

Valentine
Best Friends – Part VII

Volunteers at Best Friends are welcome to take dogs, cats, or rabbits "home" for sleepovers—whether "home" is a cabin there at the sanctuary or a hotel in the town of Kanab a few minutes away. I wasn't sure if I wanted the responsibility, even for 20 hours, after having fostered two dogs and promising myself I was just going to be selfish for the next four months before adopting again, but I couldn't pass up this part of the experience.

Before my volunteer shift at Horse Haven, I went over to Dogtown to choose my sleepover buddy. Deb, the incredibly sweet "mayor" of Dogtown, had invited me to come rather than just assigning me a dog. She introduced me to two recent arrivals, then took me over to a chunky brindle-colored pit bull-ish type dog, Valentine. The dog looked me in the eyes, her huge ears perked out to the sides, and she jumped out of her lounge chair and over to put her paws up on the half-door to say hi. We met one more dog, and I hemmed and hawed, but Deb assured me, "You're taking Valentine."

When I arrived later in the day to pick her up for the night, Deb gave me a bag with everything I needed, and off we went. I felt nervous driving her the few miles back to the cabin. She seemed anxious or excited, I wasn't sure which. I'd later learn she goes on sleepovers all the time and was way more familiar with the process than I was. (Duh.) After sniffing every inch of the cabin, she jumped up on the bed, found her spot, and calmly observed while I settled in to work. She noticed everything but was bothered by nothing.

We took a long walk along Kanab Creek through a grassy valley among the pink rock and red sand of the hills on either side. It was extremely windy, and as we walked, a massive tree split and fell right in front of us. It scared us a little, but it was quite something to witness. It felt like I was part of nature, not just a visitor, and like it was a privilege—as a human—to be allowed to be present for the tree's sudden death. I'd been enjoying day after day of solitary adventure, never feeling alone in the company of the rocks, water, and sky. But I noted how nice, how natural, it felt to have a companion of the dog sort with me now... someone to witness the tree falling with me, someone to react to the sights and sounds with. Someone to talk to, even if in silence.

At seven years old and quite a bit of heft, Valentine was pretty pooped after the long walk. She spent the whole evening snoozing on the bed...right up on my pillow I'd carefully covered with all the blankets they gave me to protect from dog hair, that she had then rearranged and gotten out of the way. I didn't care. I wrote and worked, and she snored. She apparently had distemper at some time in her life, resulting in a facial twitch. It twitches a lot when she sleeps. It's her only "quirk," and it pains me to think it's the only reason she hadn't been adopted since arriving at the Sanctuary from Mexico on Valentine's Day.

Sharing the small space with this joyful and soulful girl, I couldn't help but reflect on the dog's amazing capacity to like and to love. She didn't know me, but she was so happy with me. She wanted to snuggle. She preferred to have me in bed with her than for me to be at the table a few feet away. Just as Olive, the foster dog I'd said goodbye to before starting this trip, attached herself to me within days. As long as I was around, she was happy. These dogs had been bounced around all over the place, but rather than fear or distrust, they expressed nothing but joy to be in whatever place they are at the moment, with whomever they're with at the moment.

I also thought about Gemma, and said a prayer for her, considering what trauma must have been inflicted upon her to steal that capacity from her…a capacity that is so natural in a dog. My prayer was that she was learning what love is, that joy was breaking its way past her terror, enough that she could one day take comfort in her person and find peace in her waking hours, not just her dreams (this was before I received the update that she'd found her forever home and was thriving).

117

As I loaded up Valentine in the car to take her back to Dogtown in the morning, I began sobbing. Apparently, this is just what I do at the Sanctuary: cry. There was no part of me that wanted to adopt her. She was wonderful, just obviously not my dog. But I simply did not want to say goodbye. After Cayenne, and Gemma, and Olive, I'd reached the end of my goodbye rope. I tried to gather myself, totally embarrassed to walk inside Dogtown Headquarters such a mess. The (super-friendly…as they all are) caregiver who took her from me told me a bit about her and assured me she'd be adopted soon.

When I arrived back at my cabin, six hours later after volunteering at Cat World, it was the only moment in the entire trip when I felt lonely. I got on the Best Friends website and sponsored Valentine. I emailed Deb to ask if I could stop by to see Valentine the next day before leaving the Sanctuary. She wrote right back and said yes.

I still think about her every day. She was transported elsewhere shortly after my visit, and I have no idea where she is now. I cry as I write this. And I still can't explain why—why I got so attached to this dog I knew for such a short time, why I miss her so much. My best guess is that for me, she was the living embodiment of all that the Sanctuary is. And because this place immediately became a spiritual home for me, I'm now a little homesick all the time.

Angel's Overlook
Best Friends – Part VIII

I spent my last evening hours at the Sanctuary at Angel's Overlook. I walked a sandy one-mile trail and again marveled that I never saw another human during these soft twilight moments in this sacred place. I had heaven to myself (though I was constantly aware of all the beautiful invisible souls vibrating around me). I sat on a bench in Gratitude Garden listening to the chorus of windchimes. I wrote a letter to Cayenne. I strolled around the overlook area. I took off my locket holding Cayenne's picture and opened it. I held it up to show her the views of all the pink, blue, yellow, and red. And of course, I took a minute to sip on the vodka cocktail I'd made back in my cabin and munch on some delicious potato chips. There has never been a finer happy hour.

When numb fingers and shivers forced me to head back to the car, I moved very slowly and quietly—not my style. I paused every few steps to turn around and soak it all up. On my drive back down the road, I pulled over at one of the horse paddocks that held two horses I'd met the day before. That day, they'd had no interest in me. This night, though, they came right over to the fence. The bay enjoyed a nose rub. The white one even came in for a sniff and some photo ops. I whispered to them, and I said a wordless prayer of gratitude that a haven like this exists for them…and me. It was the perfect goodbye.

Never Alone

My week-long solo adventure was the least alone I'd felt since Cayenne died. It was the perfect cure for that mounting anxiety I'd been trying to wrangle for months—the FOMO, the feeling of caring about others more than they care about me, a desperation for connection. In my seven days away from everyone and every landscape I knew, I did not once crave the company of my friends or family. I enjoyed sending little updates to them, and I certainly leaned on family via phone/text when logistics went awry. But I felt no worry, no longing. I didn't care what was going on anywhere else. I was here. Now. And it was an immense relief. I enjoyed every minute of my own company. I felt Cayenne's spirit with me in ways more pronounced than at home, where I'm easily distracted by daily life. I took comfort in the company of the earth, wind, water, and animals. I did exactly what I wanted in any given moment—and surprisingly, given my indecision syndrome, I seemed to always know what that was.

Being somewhere new alone—traveling alone—seems to bring out the best in a lot of people—empowerment, kindness to strangers, the ability to adapt and get over mishaps quickly, a much deeper knowing of the connection to the great big world out there. Ironically, the perfect cure for loneliness just might be to get out there alone.

Dream

Before Cayenne, his was the first death of someone close to me, someone who had a huge impact on my life. Jimmy was my favorite singer-songwriter who I used to go see play at McGonigel's Mucky Duck in Houston every few months for years. Then he became my friend, and then he hired me to be his "music agent," a term he dreamed up that encompassed all things that needed doing...booking, assisting, organizing, listening to him rant about this and that for hours on end. He introduced me to a whole new world, and he introduced me to Nathan. It sends my mind reeling to think what my life would be had it not been for my friendship with Jimmy; I consider him the reason I'm now surrounded by creativity, music, nature, and many of the people I love the most. He dreamed big for me from the beginning, and he told me I was a rock star.

At night, he still visits my dreams regularly. In each one, it's understood that he's dying, and we're soaking up final moments, final hugs, final songs. Sometimes, he's weak; more and more, as time in the waking world passes, he's not.

Last night, he wasn't dying as much as we all knew he'd already left, and he was coming back to be with us for a bit. In the dreams, there's always a gig, or a festival of sorts. He loved those. There's always touching. He loved that, too. In life, we touched and hugged often, but the touch I remember most vividly is the feeling of his arm under my hand while I said goodbye to him. As I sat by the hospice bed set up in his living room, he'd held his arms up and twisted them around in the light. In total awe, he said, "I can't believe I'm lying here dying." I couldn't either.

So when he put his arms down and held one of my hands over his chest, I moved my other hand slowly and gently up and down his arm as we talked and cried. His skin was so soft. The memory is a beautiful one. It didn't matter that his physical body was a diminished version of itself. His arm felt good, and right, and familiar. The pure love pouring through his hand into mine made it excruciating to let go. He'd loved fiercely—despite his weakness—and unabashedly in the final months of his life.

Last night in the dream, we held each other and swayed while singing, "It blowed away, it blowed away, yeah my Oklahoma home has blown away..." Our arms were intertwined. His skin was soft and cool. He felt good, and right, and familiar. It went on and on. I would wake and fall back asleep and return to it. More songs, more hugs...other friends I couldn't identify, and dogs. Even his old (long-dead) brown lab showed up. It wasn't a lucid dream, just very real. At some point, we knew he'd need to leave again soon. I held on tightly and whispered, "Why can't I just know you're here all the time, even when I can't see you?" He whispered something back that gave me absolute comfort and reassurance. I tried to remember what it was when I awoke. Then he kissed me very lightly on the cheek. *Goodbye again, Jimmy. See you next time.*

I wonder why the one detail I couldn't remember from the dream is the most important: the answer, the secret. Could it be that I already know the truth, deep, deep down, where words fail?

Badass

"Damn, I seem to be in high demand!"

I said this, semi-jokingly, to Nathan the other day after receiving an email asking for my editing services—from someone who's kind of a "big deal," someone who really wanted *my* service in particular, because they knew about me. This was in the middle of one of the busiest months I've had professionally since I left the high school classroom in 2009. I gave up teaching English because, while I loved the students and relationships, it wasn't what I *really* wanted to do. I also wasn't great at it.

I'd been wandering professionally ever since, in search of just what it is I actually do want to do and how to make money doing it. (I thought my only real passion, all I ever really wanted to do, was to work with and help animals, which isn't typically a paying gig, especially when you pass out every time you try to observe a surgery when interning at a veterinary clinic.)

As I made the snarky comment about being in demand, it occurred to me that this wasn't a joke, and I need not laugh it off. I *am* in high demand. And could it be...that's actually for good reason? Could it be that I'm actually good at what I do...that I'm actually making money as a writer and editor and loving every minute of it? Could it be that I'm kind of a *badass*?

I've never felt like a badass ever in my life. Okay…not true. I felt that way once when I scored five goals in a row in what was to me a very important lacrosse game my senior year of high school. Sporty stuff has typically been the only realm where I ever came close to feeling confident, comfortable, and even a little cool. In other realms, I tended to feel like I was faking it. I assumed others knew better and did better, at whatever thing it was I was doing. I've always been willing to study hard and work hard, so I told myself that was the only reason I really had any kind of success—not ability, but work ethic. I'm guessing I'm not alone, especially as a woman. It can be natural for us to be humble and modest…to believe the myth that others are the experts…and to suffer from imposter syndrome.

For instance, for years I refused to call myself a writer (I felt like I was just acting like a writer). I'd published a book—that received recognition from several awards/festivals—and spent many hours a week writing for magazines and publications (and, again, getting paid for it). But still, I didn't dare identify myself as a writer. *Writers are people who really know what they're doing, who are really good at it, who have some magical innate creative superpower.* The thing is, though, here I am, writing. I'm doing it. And I love it just as much as I love working with the words of other real writers as an editor. So I finally learned to own it, and proudly. I am Ashley, and I'm writer and editor. Who cares if it took me until my forties to find my way to all this. And who's to say what lights me up—or what I'm good at—won't change in my fifties or sixties. I believe in myself and my ability to pursue what I want and to earn it.

I owe my ability to embrace my own badassishness in part to the amazing women, and men, I'm lucky enough to be surrounded by—people who have been open to their own evolution, who have paid attention to what doesn't feel like work and made that their work, who are courageous enough to say "yes" and *then* figure out how in the hell to do the thing they said yes to, who are committed to making the world a better place by being true to themselves and doing the things they do with the greatest of care. Making the world a better place is an essential element of "success," in my opinion; so despite carving out this career that I'm proud of, I have questioned from time to time whether my work really *matters*. Am I making the world a better place with this life of mere words and stories? When I experience that doubt, though, the universe has a way of sending me reminders and reassurances. I recently received a thank-you note from the mother of a client whose first novel I'd edited. She wrote, "You have made a huge difference in the life of someone else." *Wow!* Badass.

Tres Lunas, Tres Chicas

With the pandemic, and the isolating experience of losing Cayenne, and relational dynamics shifting as they're prone to do in a small town, this year hasn't had much to do with friends. I thrive on good friendship, on easy conversation, laughter, and hugs. Making these good friends can be quite a challenge, more so the older I get. Most of my closest friendships with girls are relationships that go back anywhere from thirty-eight (when I was five) to twenty years ago. Given how precious these are, it was a great relief to resume the annual tradition of a girls trip with Liz and Sarah, whom I've never called "Sarah" once in my life. She goes by her last name, "Flournoy," with me, just as I will always be "Stanberry" (my maiden name, my last name when I began teaching alongside her) to her.

We chose one of my favorite destinations—a resort on hundreds of acres north of Fredericksburg (Texas's version of Napa) an hour drive from my home. Liz flew from Oklahoma; Flournoy drove from Houston. Tres Lunas is an adults-only B&B with two poolside "Zen Suites," the "Sheriff's Office" where dogs are allowed to stay, and "Una Luna," a three-bedroom house down the hill, which is where the three of us stayed for three nights. Any place that allows dogs but no kids is my kind of place.

Whether it was coffee on the porch in the morning, or beers with our legs dangling in the infinity pool— Flournoy and Liz chatting up the young couple celebrating their anniversary—sipping flights of wine at a vineyard in town, or cooking dinner together in our casita, we never stopped talking. We asked challenging, thought-provoking questions of one another. We, of course, covered the confusing dynamics of all three of our marriages. We analyzed our drinking, exercise, and other habits. And we laughed through it all.

Each evening, we sat in our rockers on the sprawling porch looking out over the even-more-sprawling pasture and the lone beautiful horse grazing (a lone horse always hurts my heart...they should be among their kind). One of those evenings, the girls taught me about the "portrait" feature on the iPhone and we entertained ourselves by taking countless photos and admiring how awesome we each looked with the various filters. After cooking a delicious dinner together, working seamlessly in the kitchen as a team, we sat at the dining table until our butts got sore on the hardwood chairs, and then we kept sitting because we didn't care. The next morning, Flournoy got out her phone over breakfast, and we gut-laughed until our bellies and faces hurt because she'd filmed all these videos of me and Liz throughout the night before, just me opening a bottle of wine, Liz putting together a salad, me placing pasta on the table, Liz telling a story...quite lengthy videos. We all found it hilarious that in those wine-infused moments, Flournoy was so enamored with us that she thought we were worthy of these mini-films. She does love us so.

These are the kinds of friends you never tire of... because they don't suck energy, they foster it. There are no misunderstandings, no need to carefully choose words, no need for politeness or putting anything on. We simply and purely enjoy each other's company and truly want happiness for one another. We believe in the gifts we each bring to the world and encourage each other to share those gifts. Not everyone is lucky enough to have these kinds of friends, and they are a constant reason to be grateful.

Endings Are Not Erasers
Galveston – Part I

Nathan and I came to Galveston to work on a book we've been co-writing. The concept is that we developed a long list of topics, and over a year or two we each wrote about them separately, without any discussion or sharing. In my humble opinion, it's kind of a fascinating window into the vast differences in the way we think about certain things (friendships, a particular argument we had, God…) as well as the deep similarities—some that drew us together early on, some that we developed over the years. It's not that we are fascinating as individuals. It's just an interesting study in relationship, the types of things that connect us, and the endless things we'll never really understand about one another…all of us. It's a challenging project, though, to work on over a long period of time—time that has a way of changing how we think about certain things. I fear that it will be in an endless state of editing.

We also came here because it's only a four-hour drive, we have a place to stay, and because having grown up in Houston, Galveston is an old friend of mine. In her first year with me, Cayenne came to Galveston along with my first husband and his dog. I don't actually remember the experience—which kills me; I often curse my limited memory, especially when it comes to her, but my little pea brain can only carry so much data. I have photographs, though, of her sitting happily in the sand with her tongue hanging about eight inches out of her mouth. I wouldn't be able to count all the places she went with me over fifteen years. I wouldn't be able to count all the places I've been with Nathan, either. So much life lived with both...so many adventures. As I contemplate conclusions, endings, goodbyes—some unavoidable; some chosen— my experiences with Cayenne (even the ones I don't consciously remember) remind me that an end does nothing to negate the value of all we did together, all that love. It all becomes part of us. Endings are not erasers.

This is a reminder I could really benefit from applying to my human relationships. Throughout my life I've been extremely reluctant to end romances, including that first marriage (that I knew deep down was the wrong thing even when I accepted the proposal), and a couple of toxic friendships with people who behaved monstrously. My good, healthy friends have questioned what in the world my deal breakers are— why I hold onto people that not only hurt me but clearly have a pattern of poisoning most everyone they touch (despite their charm, magnetism, and humor that lure you in). I couldn't think of any deal breakers. I literally could not think of one behavior that would lead me to confidently and gladly say, Enough... Done...Goodbye. My justification has been two-fold: it seems so wasteful—of the time, energy, and love expended in the relationship; and, it's just sad, having to throw away the good stuff along with the garbage. Basically, I'd miss them.

This inability of mine to accept the temporal nature of relationships does not extend to animals, though. I know many loving souls who have lost an animal and refuse to adopt again, solely because they don't want to go through the pain of saying goodbye. Despite my ridiculous holding-on tendencies, I don't get this one. Death, to me, is a very different kind of ending. It's inevitable, and therefore somehow less tragic, the heartbreak more tolerable. Trying to avoid the grief that comes with the death of the ones we love would mean avoiding love altogether. What a shame, I think, to miss out on years and years of the purest kind of love there is—that we share with our animals—because we are too scared to grieve.

Seabird
Galveston – Part II

The birds out here are mesmerizing—the cute little ones that shuffle along the sand, the gulls, and the pelicans. As I watch the different birds go about their day from my various vantage points on the beach and in the water, I'm struck by how well they all *transition*. From sky to water to land. Dry to wet. Hot to cold. Calm to stormy to really stormy. They seem unfazed. Every movement is graceful. Meanwhile, I typically take about twenty minutes to ease myself into a chilly body of water, squealing with every inch I go deeper— and this awkward "squealing" applies to my attitude about change in any form.

I want to be more like a seabird.

An afternoon spent envying these birds led me to return to my animal spirit wisdom research. I wondered what the gulls and pelicans had to teach me. Seagulls represent freedom, independence, and *the possibility of living your life without feeling alone.* When a seagull comes into your awareness, it could be reminding you of your uniqueness and self-sufficiency and *that you can have your way of life without loneliness.* The gull also inspires passion and to never stop seeking what lights you up. As a spirit animal, because of its connection to water, the gull offers perspective, particularly of one's emotional landscape (water is related to emotion)—helping us to understand what's best for our well-being.

Pelicans, also as much at home in the water as the sky, symbolize adaptability and creativity. When they cross your path, they can remind you that even if you're going through a difficult time, or change, that you can adapt and you will be okay. I was surprised to learn that in the Christian tradition, they symbolize sacrifice and resurrection. Also, due to their role in burials and funerals in ancient Egypt, they are associated with the afterlife; some believe the appearance of a pelican is a message from a deceased loved one reassuring you that they're okay, and that it's time to move beyond your grief.

Both of these bird spirits encourage us to look at the bigger picture and to know that we will find happiness in exploring new horizons, especially once we learn to love our solitude; for it is only then that we can embrace our personal power, better express ourselves, and love without becoming overly attached in our relationships. It seems my mesmerization has been warranted...that I really do need to become more like a seabird.

Salt Water
Galveston – Part III

Two years ago, while snorkeling just off the Bermuda coast, I swam for a few moments with a sea turtle in the warm, crystal-clear waters—waters so salty that my body stayed afloat with almost no effort. Because Cayenne was alive, but "old," I only allowed myself to join my dad's special retirement gift to the whole family celebration trip for three nights, which was fine, because all I needed were those moments in that water, with that turtle. It was pure peace. My mind was silent. Nothing but breath and a water dance with a creature who made his home in this salty paradise.

Here in Galveston, the Gulf waters are not crystal clear. They are so murky I wouldn't be able to spot a turtle one foot away. But still...there's something about salt water. It starts as soon as my feet touch the tiny waves breaking at my ankles. Once I'm fully in— which the soothing bathtub temp waters make it easy to do quickly—I'm fully there. Or here, now. The little fish darting all around me and the wads of seaweed that brush up against me and startle me every time are not quite the meditative companions the sea turtle was. But still...

When I swim away from the shore, and all I can see is the vastness of the water, the sky, the seagulls, and the fish leaping out of the water as they feed, I am just...

happy. All worries disappear. All thoughts of past and future become irrelevant. I don't know if everyone feels this way, or if I must've lived another life as a creature of the sea. Outside of jaunts to this area, I didn't grow up spending much time in or around beaches or salt water. I was more into horses than fish, turtles, or birds. So I'm intrigued by how at-home I feel when immersed in ocean waters, and how I felt with that Bermuda turtle. Of course, I also feel at home in the Colorado mountains, and I learned of a home I never knew I had at Best Friends in Utah. If I begin to put these pieces of seemingly different puzzles together, I start to see an absolutely beautiful, albeit abstract, work of art. Maybe the pieces actually do belong to the same puzzle, and when I complete it, I will see an image of home that is full of dogs, cats, oceans, mountains, horses, prairies and pastures, lightning and storm clouds, sunshine, canyons, bears, birds, yellow flowers, trees, rivers, foxes, even snakes…oh, and me. I'm there, too.

Storms
Galveston – Part IV

A seemingly paradoxical trait of mine is how much I love storms—weather in general, really. I love the excitement of action: hurricanes, blizzards, lightning, thunder—the wonder and beauty of nature on display. You'd think that given my sometimes debilitating discomfort with change, along with the fact that storms can cause destruction and even death—to fragile animals as well as humans—that I'd be a California weather kind of person: sunny and 70s all the time... safe. Nope. Despite being home-bound and losing water for days, and the knowledge that people were suffering all over Texas, I personally soaked up every minute of the "Snowmageddon" we experienced in February. It was different, and it was exciting.

Outside of the "500-year flood" of 2015 (truly devastating; I must say, I didn't enjoy that particular weather event) and the big snowy freeze this year, we don't get a lot of super exciting weather in the Hill Country. But here now, I'm sitting on the second-story porch (everything in Galveston is "second-story" because, of course, on the coast one always has to prepared for these "exciting" weather events). At cocktail hour, a storm blew in out of nowhere, after a scorching sunny day. I've been watching and feeling it for an hour, and it's wonderful. The shelter of the porch is allowing me to sit and write while winds rage all around me. The sky is blue, white, gray, and off toward the horizon a pink-lavender with streaks of lightning bolting through. There is no movie, no concert that could enrapture me more. This is my preferred mode of entertainment—the smells of salt and water on the hot pavement, sounds of palm trees whooshing and American flags whipping, the taste of salt not only from the air but from this margarita I'm sipping on, the invigorating sensation of wind and moisture on my sunburnt skin, and the birds seeming to enjoy the ride along the rollercoaster of wind.

I guess what it comes down to is that my fear of boredom outweighs my fear of change. I cannot be bored in the middle of a storm. Maybe that's why I'm still married.

Tearing It Down
Galveston – Part V

While we lay on chaise lounges on the porch of the
bay house in Sea Isle, having spent an afternoon
working on our book project years in the making
(much to the dismay of my impatient nature), Nathan
teared up. They were happy tears of healing, he
explained. The sunset, the afternoon of doing what we
love, taking breaks to swim in the ocean and sip on
salty Coronas…they were working their magic on
him. He seemed to be reassuring both me and himself,
that he is, in fact, healing. From what isn't really
important. Well, I'm sure it's immensely important to
him. But it's lost its importance to me. I'm losing my
compassion for his pain and my patience for his
healing. And this breaks my heart, for both of our
sakes. Especially after a chunk of days like this, when
we settle in the space of all we have in common and
remember what it's like to just have a little fun.

All these years, we've both been a home for one
another, or we've tried. We made a family with Cayenne, with all six of our parents (including "steps")
and his daughter, and then Stoney and Dylan. But a
home is supposed to be a shelter (rather than the
storm itself), a soft place to fall where you are accepted
just as you are. So what do you do when you find that
the home you've been building and nesting in for
fourteen years has cracks in the foundation and mold

growing in the attic—you love this home, but it's no longer safe for its inhabitants. While it's one thing never to be bored in a relationship, it's taking it a little far to live on edge, fearing that at some point the roof of your home may come crashing down on you both.

We've tried so hard, and we love each other as much as we ever have—but it may be that fixing foundation cracks and eradicating mold are beyond our skills. Even as we work to more fully accept one another, to learn how to communicate without blame and defensiveness, to sweep away all the eggshells we've been used to walking on and around, I don't know that we can fix the damage we've done to the structure. It may be that the most loving, healthy thing to do is tear down the house, and rebuild. Whether we can make a new, healthy home together, or if we have to do it separately, I do not know. For that moment on the porch, the best I could do is accept the not knowing and look forward to one last swim in those murky, magical, salty waters before heading back to a different kind of home.

A request for a little grace from readers...

At this point in the book, I feel the need to pause and acknowledge the complicated nature of including personal details about Nathan and *our* story. One of the difficulties is that he's not getting to share *his* story, in this book at least (he is an author, so he tells his own stories when and how he wants). It's one thing for me to share vulnerable realities of my own life; another altogether to share his—especially when all you're getting are those "realities" through my perspective...which calls into question if there even is a reality, or only the stories we tell ourselves and others. It's fascinating how two people can theoretically experience the exact same moment, but their individual retellings of that moment would have little in common. And once a moment is gone, all we have are memories, colored by the lens through which we originally viewed the experience in addition to our unique values, emotions, and biases. It'd be easy to spend days—or a lifetime, really—pondering the potential non-existence of reality, similar to the non-existence to time. But it makes my pea brain hurt, so I'll get back to my point...

The trouble here is that our two stories are so intertwined, and Nathan was such a big part of this "year of travel" and all it entailed, that I have not been able to find a way to tell my truth—my supposed reality—without including him as a "main character."

Rest assured, he read every word before publication and, though he remembers certain moments differently, or would explain things differently, he acknowledges that this is my story, and he's okay with it. More than that, he's been nothing but supportive of this book, and all of my writing endeavors, along the way.

I appreciate your graceful understanding of the delicate nature of all the sharing of all the stories.

Ready

"We are laced into our DNA, environment, families of origin, friends and lovers, all of mankind, the unfathomable mystery of being. Life is both a conscious and unconscious lacing of the heart, mind, and body to people, places, rituals, philosophies, and objects. Ultimately the lacing impresses upon the soul, even as it remains pure in its original form. When we believe we are undoing the laces, even severing them, there are knots that will withstand not only our singular will, but also eternity. And what we perceive as 'good' is always laced with what we perceive as 'bad.' Beauty is laced with pain. Our pain is laced with grace."

~ *Lise Liddell, Liner Notes, "Laced"*

Ten months after her death—a little premature given my promise to myself to take a year, and given the one last big trip planned (I mean, this all had to culminate in Montana)—I found myself unable to stop looking at adoptable dogs online. My heart was both full— with the cats and foster dogs and Cayenne's spirit— and still broken. But a heart, after all, is not a container with a point at the bottom and two humps that cracks down the middle when it breaks or grows a few sizes like the Grinch's when it's bursting with love. It's never at capacity. It's shapeless and infinite, even when broken. And mine felt a dog out there somewhere calling.

For months, I'd been getting regular emails from Adopt-a-Pet, a site that matches your search criteria to dogs in shelters and rescue organizations within a certain radius, a site I honestly don't recall activating or providing any search criteria for. Now that I was opening the emails, it became a fun way to avoid work, looking at all these adorable pups and wondering. It was also a bit agonizing and terrifying...the impending decision-making, the not knowing, the search for the dog that would need to check off all the boxes on my impossible wish-list:

- ♥ Love the cats
- ♥ Zero predatory instincts
- ♥ Great road companion (no car-sickness)
- ♥ Jog with me (no pulling)
- ♥ No licking
- ♥ Smart, quiet, and gentle
- ♥ Enjoy alone time without separation anxiety
- ♥ Sleep until 10 a.m.
- ♥ Loyal and affectionate
- ♥ Generally perfectly behaved
- ♥ Fill the space that's existed in our home and family since Cayenne died

With all the wondering, it seemed like we should at least go meet one, just to see what it felt like. So one afternoon, Nathan and I headed out to PAWS. I told myself and him that this was just an experiment. Totally casual. But two minutes into the drive, I found

myself crying. It felt like I was leaving something—
like I was leaving her—behind.

The pup was sweet and lovely. But she barked at cats,
and she was still very much a puppy. I spent all
evening fretting over what had to be a really quick
decision because she was in high demand. I couldn't
commit (that hadn't been the plan anyway), and
someone else snatched her up the next morning. It
was too much emotionally, so I dropped the search
for a while. A very little while. But more emails came.
I filled out applications with various rescue groups in
the area. I scrolled through photos and bios. This was
now an inevitable part of my daily life; I couldn't stop
no matter what my head told me.

One day I found myself on the phone with the head
of the Spay and Neuter Initiative for Pets of San
Antonio, or SNIPSA. I'd seen a couple of dogs of
interest on their website. This woman took time out
of her very busy day to talk to me at length about what
I was looking for. She told me about "Caramel," not
one of the dogs I'd called about. I'd seen her on the
site, but I thought she was out of my desired size
range. I was told she was really special, particularly
"chill." She was the only dog they'd ever been able to
keep in the office and let roam free. She just hung out
by an employee's desk, unperturbed by all the puppies
and goings-on. That sounded like the gentle, non-
predatory cat-lover I was looking for. I was intrigued.

I went to meet this blonde, goofy-looking girl with ears like Yoda. I admit that no angels sang; there was no magical knowing. But she was cute and happy…a little more interested in her chewie than me…and after leaving, I couldn't get her off my mind. By the time Nathan got back in town two days later, I'd lined up yet another pup to check out on our way to meet Caramel together. With all these meet-n-greets and a life-changing decision ahead, I wrote to Cayenne that morning. I told her this was hard—this moving on… and that only she could help me. I told her I'd need a sign, plain and simple. I explained what the sign should be if the little black pup, our first stop, was the one. We ended up spending a lot of time with this timid, gentle sweetheart—who definitely got to me— but Cayenne delivered no signs before, after, or during. When it came to Caramel, I'd given Cayenne three options: a rainbow (that's a tall order, which is why I gave her options), a feather during our visit, or a Cayenne-style stretch (she had particular ways of moving) from the dog.

Caramel was now in a foster home. When we walked through the front door, the first thing Nathan did was scratch her chest like he used to with Cayenne. She immediately stretched her head up way toward the sky cocking her neck in a long curve, and we both said out loud, "Cayenne." (Note: She's never stretched like that since. She prefers scratches in other places.) We took her into the yard and walked over to a bench. She picked up something in the grass and set it back down. I asked, "Whatcha got there?" It was a feather, gray with a blue stripe. At that point, I told Nathan about my letter to Cayenne, and the signs I'd prayed for. On the way home, we pretty much decided it'd be a big middle finger to the universe to ignore the fact that I asked, and my angel delivered. So, Caramel it would be. (But, of course, that was not her real name. I knew what her name was, though I forced myself to wait to give it to her, to be sure.)

The evening before we went to pick her up, a huge downpour blew in out of nowhere. We'd been gathering wood for an outdoor fire when this unpredicted storm blew in and we had to run inside. The rain stopped as quickly as it came in, and a few minutes later the skies were bright blue again. I went to the backdoor, secretly thinking what a miracle it would be if there was a rainbow...specifically out over the shed, where I once took a photo of Cayenne lying in the yard with a rainbow overhead. And there it was. The third sign. It was then that I committed to the name that I'd picked out years before, after I heard my dear friend's song, "Laced with Grace," on her album entitled "Laced." Lacey it would be.

"Little Fox and Tiny Bird"

The same dear friend—my fairy god-sister as I call her—wrote this song for me and Cayenne days after she died. As soon as she could make it from Houston, Lise came over and sang it a capella out at Cayenne's grave. Every time I listen to this song, which she's now recorded for her latest album, I am blown away by how *seen* I feel. I don't know that I ever spoke to Lise about my obsession with Stoney's paws. But she watches and listens and knows me to my core. She's always understood my cats and dogs are my children, my ultimate connection to this vast universe. I felt compelled to include the lyrics here, to help convey what a loving, compassionate soul my sweet Lise is and why I would want to name my new family member after her song.

Little fox and tiny bird
Sleepy fawn and frisky squirrel
Autumn leaves and summer hail
Stoney's paws and Cayenne's tail

Fish inside the river swim
Butterfly lights on your skin
Oh, the glow is there within
Whatever ends, begins again

A million universes swirl
Tiny lives in this vast world

I fear that I may never cease
To weep beside your grave my sweet
I so will miss your wagging tail
As we skipped along your trail

For you were always leading me
Joyfully and patiently
O'er the hills and through the dales
Never missing one detail

A million universes swirl
Tiny lives in this vast world

But now lady bugs and dinosaurs
Pee wee crabs on sandy shores
Coax me into needed sleep
And tuck our memories 'tween the sheets

A million universes swirl
Tiny lives in this vast world
A million universes twirl
Tiny lives in this vast world

The Day We Picked Her Up

For a week, I'd been all preparation and nesting and prayer. Praying that this would be the right dog, that I would do all the rights things to raise her, that we would find a home in and with one another. That morning, I'd spent some quiet time at Cayenne's grave, preparing my energy to be calm and confident. I knew our new girl would pick up on the energy I was carrying. And I wanted to be good for her, on this momentous first day of our life together.

Nathan had been distantly interested in the whole process. In a rare moment of enthusiasm and decisiveness, on that day when she picked up the feather and gave me the sign, he agreed that we should bring her home—we should adopt her and just see, especially since the rescue group offers a seven-day "grace period." (Like I would ever "return" a dog I've committed to…)

A month or so earlier, we'd devoted a two-hour therapy session to our different ways of being with animals, when I began to feel like it was time to look for another dog, and as I sought the answer to whether this would be "my" dog or "our" dog. I came to understand that Nathan *respects* every animal life, but *love*…that takes him time. He'd never loved another dog like he did Cayenne. She loved and accepted him unconditionally, made him smile, and often brought him out of his own head with her quiet but caring presence. It took him many years to feel that love, and to accept all the dog hair in all the places that came along with it and her. I think it was also easier to love her once she'd settled into a low-maintenance dog who required little other than easy walks and ear scratches. She was smart, gentle, and intuitive and didn't need much "correcting" or training. She liked her personal space—wasn't much of a snuggler, and definitely not a licker. These were qualities that appealed to him.

Despite the differences in how we relate to animals (I don't mind them all up in my business, and I tend to fall in love quickly), we'd agreed in that therapy session that we both wanted to be in on the adoption and training of a new dog together, as much as his travel schedule would allow. This would be *our* dog. And we agreed I'd have to be patient while he develops love for her at his own turtle-pace. And once we'd chosen Lacey, we discussed and agreed on the day to bring her home, I had thought.

Ten minutes into the drive to San Antonio, though— just far enough to not be able to turn around (so I could ditch Nathan and do this myself), he began huffing and puffing. He'd been looking at his phone since getting in the car. I asked what was wrong. This is what was wrong: Of all days, this was THE day he needed to be home working. He'd just started a Patreon account, and it wasn't functioning properly on his phone. He hadn't reconciled things with

Cayenne. He didn't want to be going to get this dog. He wasn't ready. This isn't where he wanted to be. Well, shit.

All my preparation—within and without—was for naught. I couldn't believe we were about to put a sweet, tentative dog—with no reason to trust us or where we were taking her—into our car, with all this...this anger, this fear, this not-wanting. Of course I could empathize with his fear—I know (especially now, in hindsight) that he was just nervous, because he had no idea how this new relationship would go, no idea if this dog would like him, no guarantees of anything, really. But I couldn't empathize with how and when he chose to express it. I didn't have words for my disappointment or my own anger, so we drove on in silence. As I wept quietly, he did interrupt the silence to gently promise to gather himself before we arrived, to try to be good for her.

For the rest of the drive, I wondered. I wondered if dogs wonder. I wondered what she would be thinking as these two strangers took her off into the unknown. And I wondered if I could do this...if I could forgive Nathan for allowing his doubt to override his ability to be there for me, or for her, on one of the most important days of my life...I wondered if maybe I do have some deal breakers after all.

Lacey Puppy

She'd been picked up by Animal Control wandering the small town of Lockhart, Texas, when she was six months old. I don't know a thing about her first months on this earth. I'd also adopted Cayenne when she was six months old, having been picked up on the streets of Houston as a stray. Lacey looks nothing like Cayenne, though I'd been sure I wanted another cattle-dog mix—spotty tan and black with those pointy, perky ears. Instead, she's five shades of blonde and white with gigantic pink and black paw pads. Her ears were like huge wings when I met her. One is settling down and flopping more; the other still sticks out to the side. They're both very soft. She has two white socks on her wolf-like front feet. Lacey "Two Socks" Brown.

She regularly rolls over to expose her belly, something Cayenne *never* did. She licks (see "impossible wish list" point five). When she lies down to relax and watch the world, she crosses her front paws daintily. She rolls to and fro on the rug with glee and throws her toys in the air for herself to catch. She particularly liked a stuffed frog that croaks and croaks and croaks...and croaks. Ultimately, though, she kills all of her toys. Cayenne's toys lasted for months, if not years. She destroyed nothing. Lacey is more physical in all the ways, including her desire to snuggle. It's new to me, and I kind of love it.

Her brown eyes, somehow both deeply dark and bright, are complemented by delicate but lush blonde eyelashes. Her shiny jet-black lips and the thick black outline of her eyes make it look like she's wearing lipstick and eyeliner. She could be a model. Her smile reveals perfect, big, white teeth, like Cayenne never had due to her bout with distemper as a pup that hindered her teeth from ever developing protective enamel. She's all leg and hip and sits awkwardly and adorably like a puppy…she *is* a puppy, even if she's over thirty-five pounds already.

Outside of the house or yard, she is timid and freezes at every new sight and sound. There was a white truck parked down the road this morning. She would not walk that way. She growled at the small metal buffalo in the spirit garden by the fire pit. A gust of wind makes her jump. In the safety of the fenced backyard, she lets loose, though. Her abundance of playful, observant energy makes me nervous about the cats, whom I've not let her officially meet yet. I'm not sure what happened to the "chillness" she exhibited in the care of the rescue group. With them, she reacted to nothing. With us, she reacts to everything. She's obviously going to be a cat chaser, the one thing I'd feared (see "impossible with list" points one and two). But I'm trying not to worry.

I'm always tired because she doesn't let me sleep past eight (see "impossible wish list" point eight). Cayenne always slept in with me as late as I wanted, never making a peep. I cry from time to time; I knew I would.

It's hard having a dog in the house who I don't yet know, and who does not know me. I remind myself that I also cried for weeks when I brought puppy Cayenne home in July of 2005. It was the exact same. She was crazy. She was reactive. She had no reason to be loyal to me or to listen. I had no idea who she would become, who we would become…that she was my soul-dog. I had no idea the adventures we would share. So I ask for angel Cayenne to help me be patient as Lacey and I learn about each other, and to remember we can have multiple soul mates in a lifetime…and then I jump up to open the door so Lacey, who now has the crazies and is running circles around the house, kicking up rugs, can bound outside.

Big Sky
Montana – Part I

I've dreamed of going to Montana for about three decades. In my head, it's always seemed like perfection: wide open space, mountains, horses, forests, rivers, lakes, and of course, the big sky. So despite swearing off flying after the fiasco that was fourteen hours to get to Arizona, I booked my last trip of the "year of travel." There's no driving to Montana from Wimberley, unless you have a couple extra weeks to spare. And now that a dog was again part of my life, I didn't have that. We adopted Lacey three weeks ago, so it's back to the guilt and worry that come along with travel when our pup has to be left behind.

We actually arrived at our destination—Kalispell, Montana—hours ahead of schedule. Unheard of. The four hours we'd spent in the air were tolerable, but barely. In contrast to the utopia we were flying toward, every so often my stomach would turn when I thought about what hell (if I believed in hell) might be: a never-ending flight with turbulence, a crying baby, a normal-sized man in the seat beside me but who appears ginormous as he spills over into my space because airplane seats are not made for humans but for some unknown tiny creatures that don't have legs and enjoy sitting so upright that their heads are actually being pushed slightly forward, blaring commercials and music United Airlines forces upon passengers in the cabin before take-off, and a stream of TV screens on the backs of every seat, all showing different things. It's a test of sanity, for sure.

After leaving the charming Glacier International Airport in Kalispell to board the Enterprise shuttle and confirming the $750 I'd be spending on our rental car, the moment of relief arrived: we were handed the keys, and we were now free. Free to move about however we chose. Free to travel in peace and quiet. Free to rest our asses and feet in a slightly more human-appropriate position for the remainder of our journey. Now I could breathe it in—I'd made it to Montana.

Fire and Smoke
Montana – Part II

Unfortunately, what I was breathing in was mostly smoke. The minute we stepped out of the airport, it was obvious the whole state was on fire. I was over-whelmed with the smell of smoke, and the sky was nothing but a grey-yellowy-orange haze in every direction. My stomach sank. Isn't the entire point of being in Montana the views, the fresh air, the deep blue of the sky against the yellow and green of the prairies and purple outline of mountains? Where was all that?

The rental car guy said it was really bad today, with the wind, and that we might get a better hour here and there...but that, yes, fire was everywhere. Apparently, quite typical for July. Nobody had told me that! As we drove through the little town of Kalispell, I was quiet—trying to be cool. I finally made it to Montana, my last hurrah of my big year, and it was nothing but haze. I was grateful that Nathan, after he'd been working to absorb the same reality, offered some confident comfort, saying we'd simply make the best of it, that we'd enjoy what we could see up close, and that surely we'd get some days when the wind shifted.

I don't have a single photo from the trip where the landscape isn't shrouded in that hazy smoke—and it's not like we stuck to one area. One of my primary factors when deciding where in the great state to travel and be was to avoid people, and this is not just because of the pandemic. That's just generally my goal. Most people I know who've been to Montana of course spent at least some time in Yellowstone (that's the whole "attraction"). But their stories, along with every single internet source, about the crowds made my skin crawl. Standstill traffic and nothing but taillights on the most scenic drive through the park? Um…no. To me, "traffic" and "scenic" cannot co-exist. The only other national park I'd been to was our jaunt to Big Bend the previous fall. I was happy to see it, yes, but I couldn't get on board with experiencing the pristine beauty of nature surrounded by people. On the more popular hikes, you had to step off the trail every ten seconds or so to let hikers coming the other way get by. When we'd gotten to the big window at the end of The Window Trail, the view through the "window" was obscured by multiple teens sprawled about, uninterested in moving or sharing. There was no place to sit in silence to enjoy a snack and beer. We were listening to other people's conversations the entire time. So, while I'd often wondered why this outdoorsy nature-lover hadn't been to more national parks, I wondered no more. I don't know if it's snooty or selfish or just weird, but these amusement park-like crowds and atmosphere sort of spoil the whole point of the experience for me.

After all of my research, then, I decided we could handle Glacier National Park. My brother—a world traveler with no aversion to people—had given me a gift card for Under Canvas, a national park "glamping" experience, so I had to try. We'd spend two nights there before driving down to the Ennis area and keeping our explorations to non-park areas/trails. It was cool to stay in a "tent" with a comfy king bed, running water, and electricity. But it was right on the main road into the park, so there was constant road noise, and it required socializing with strangers in the common area as snacks were not allowed in the tents (that would essentially be inviting a bear to join you in bed). Glacier was stunningly beautiful, and thanks to the advice of the sweet young girls running Under Canvas, we managed to find a trail on which we only passed by one group of three hikers. The six-hour drive to our next destination would have also been stunningly beautiful, as it took us past lake after lake, but they were difficult to make out, even just fifty yards away. So instead, it was all just kind of eerie. There was not a chance of seeing any mountains, and the sun was a sad pale yellow little ball hiding behind a smoldering sky. It was a little heartbreaking, but we laughed it off.

Whining and moaning wouldn't have changed a thing. Like Steinbeck says, you can't really enjoy travel until you accept that you're not taking the trip, the trip is taking you. This trip didn't take me to the spectacular views I'd envisioned, but it did take me to a remote cabin on a gorgeous ranch where we'd spend the remainder of the week, and where we enjoyed the constant entertainment of a bird mom and dad working together to feed their babies in their nest in the cabin porch rafters. Every fifteen minutes or so, day after day, a parent would make a delivery and the babies would raise their little heads out of the nest, peeping raucously until they'd gotten their share. Sometimes all you need is a porch in the middle of nowhere with a nest of birds. Plus, the fires just gave me an excuse to come back.

Horse

The wide-open spaces, mountains, forests, rivers, lakes, and big sky may have all been shrouded in smoke. But that one most important association I have with Montana is horses, and they did not disappoint. It was a given we'd need to ride. While I was making plans months before, I looked into riding at the ranch where we were staying as well as a few other options. They were all about $200 per person, and I knew they'd be the semi-boring typical trail ride kind of situation...with strangers. No thanks. Then I remembered our friend James McMurtry had mentioned riding with a friend of his up there whenever he was on tour in the area. He gave me her name and number, and upon mentioning his name to her via text, she very happily put us on her schedule for a very reasonable price.

A few minutes into meeting Cress, I knew I liked her. She was tough but sweet, a horse person through and through, married to a cowboy. As we made our way up the mountain on our reliable mounts, she shared stories about Montana weather and horses, and we shared stories about the Austin live music scene. She'd met James after one of his shows—they'd got to talkin' horses, and she offered to take him for a ride. We laughed about the very few topics that will spark this reticent man's interest: horses, guns, the road, and fishing. Once we reached the peak, we gave the horses a rest (they'd worked pretty hard to get us up there), soaked in the quiet and the limited views of the surrounding smoky (not to be confused with Great Smoky) mountains, and headed back down. Between stories, I reveled in the sound of the leather saddles creaking and hooves meeting the ground. The feeling of being on the back of a horse—the trust involved, the power underneath you, the sensation of their movement—is like nothing else.

Back at the ranch that evening, though, we wandered out to a huge pasture during sunset. At the far end stood two black horses. Just as we spied them, they began to gallop across the pasture. It was clear they didn't have a destination in mind. They were just running to run. And it was one of the most beautiful things I've ever seen. Yes, I love to ride, but to witness a horse running wild and free, no saddle or bridle, through the pastures of Montana…well, that was it. I got what I came for.

While I've been a rider since I was ten, I haven't spent much time with horses just being horses. Given that it seems so obvious that horses represent freedom and power, and that I encounter them so often, I'd never stopped to dig deeper into what the Horse Spirit has to share with us. Witnessing the running black horses was such an enchanting moment that I decided to get out my trusty animal spirit oracle card deck, wondering what particular wisdom lay there for me. When this spirit appears, it signifies this is a time for travel and adventure, whether literal or in the sense of making choices—understanding you are *free* to choose. A social animal, the horse reminds us that help and companionship will be available wherever we choose to go. *Life is an adventure, and Horse Spirit wants you to know that whatever choices you make, you have Great Spirit within.* I couldn't hold back the tears as I read. I immediately had a vision of being on the back of one of those black horses, while she runs as fast as she can, and all I have to do is think it, and she heads in the direction I have chosen. I'm wild and free, capable of making difficult choices, and yet I'm not alone. I'm one with this powerful companion who is helping me get to where I need to go.

If you happen to have an inquiry about a relationship when Horse Spirit appears to you, it's telling you to make a move...make a choice, and let go of the need to control. Just enjoy the freedom. Enjoy the ride.

Becoming a Silence Junkie
Montana – Part III

"Let us be silent, that we may hear the whispers of the gods."

~ Ralph Waldo Emerson

Growing up in Houston, manmade noise was all around. In our home, TVs were always on. My parents had one in their bedroom, my brother had one, I had one; there was one in the study, one in the living room, and one in the kitchen. That's a lot of TVs for four people. And this was back when you couldn't fast-forward through commercials, which as we all know, are at a much louder volume than programs (who says "programs" anymore? I'm keeping this in because it makes me laugh at my old-lady self). I played outside a lot, but there was always distant road noise and so...much...lawn maintenance. None of it bothered me, that I was aware of. Noise was all I knew.

I've now lived in the Texas Hill Country—in the "Dark Sky" community of Wimberley—for nine years. When we first came here, we bought a home tucked way back in a neighborhood, with only one neighbor, surrounded by woods. I began to, unknowingly, detox from noise. As that occurred, every noise slowly became more and more obvious, more and more disturbing. Since so few cars drove by, I noticed every single one and would always look out the window, feeling irritated when one dared to disturb my workday or my general serenity.

In this neighborhood that was developing at the speed of a microwavable bag of popcorn, the noise increased on a daily basis. The new homes and all the cars, and people working on those cars in their driveways, encroached farther and farther into what had been such a quiet space. And I began to lose my mind. Somewhere along the way, it seems I became a silence junkie. I crave it. I need it. I'm a little caught off guard by this new addiction. Just as I've always appreciated the wisdom of being still so that you may know God, without being able to live it, I've *believed* in the knowledge of, "Listen to silence. It has so much to say," but I'd not lived it.

Throughout most of my life, I've sought out movement or "doing" along with some amount of noise to keep me company in my alone time (or even to buffer time with others, lest there be awkward silence). Now, though, finally, I've begun to listen to the silence, and I'm hooked on what is has to say. I've reached a point where I'm unable to stand the noise of commercials, an F-150 firing up, pounding base music coming from a neighbor's pool party. The noises not only make me angry, but they literally feel painful. The aural assault of a siren or a leaf blower will send me over the edge.

In her last weeks, if Cayenne wasn't sleeping, all she wanted to do was stand in the backyard, or wander the spirit garden, in silence. It seemed to me like she was listening to something, and like she was comforted by what she was hearing. Stoney will often meow and meow at me until I finally just settle down into a still position, so he can hop on my lap, and we can just sit in silence. Their influence, and the luxury of living where I can be in the quiet of nature so often, has had a profound impact on me. And now I'm on a crusade to encourage people (especially my friends and family who live in Houston, whom I feel like I need to save!) to seek out the sound of silence. Here's some stuff I dug up on what good it might do us—spiritually, mentally, physically, and emotionally:

- **Reduction of anxiety due to increased mindfulness:** Being fully aware, in the here and now, in any given moment, rather than trying (even subconsciously) to process stimuli, can calm us. The opportunity for increased *self*-awareness—what's going on inside rather than outside—can also increase our self-compassion. More self-compassion can lead to greater compassion in general.
- **Increased brain function:** Studies suggest silence can promote brain cell growth and cognitive processing.
- **Improved physical wellness:** Silence helps to decrease stress hormones, lower blood

pressure, decrease heart rate, and reduce muscle tension.

- **Creativity and concentration:** We are much more likely to get into that creative *flow* without the distraction of noise. Even if we think we are tuning out the noise, our brains are processing it, meaning we're not fully engaged in what we're doing.

- **Spiritual well-being:** It is only in silence that we can listen to ourselves, to our souls, to Spirit or God. Listening to our inner voice, allowing us to know and be our true selves, is the only way to experience true peace.

Highly Sensitive Dog
Montana – Part IV

Years ago, I applied to be the copyeditor for two digital publications: Introvert, Dear and Highly Sensitive Refuge. I didn't get that job, but I did a lot of reading on the sites and wrote a couple of pieces for them. I'd always known I'm your typical introvert, but this whole "highly sensitive people" (HSP) thing was new to me. First learning about it felt like that moment in "A Charlie Brown Christmas" when Lucy suggests Charlie might have pantaphobia (the fear of everything), and he exclaims, "That's it!" with such enthusiasm that Lucy is flipped backwards from her chair. But my internal exclamation was, "That's *Nathan*!" The story I ended up writing for them was "Seven Keys to a Happy Marriage with an HSP."

I'm now realizing that I, myself, am becoming an HSP, *and* it turns out we've adopted an HSD, a highly sensitive dog. Everything startles Lacey and seems to cause her anxiety and hesitation: a leaf, a deer, and especially construction noise, lawn equipment, and cars—anything new and relatively unnatural. One day while trying to encourage her around the block on a hot, humid, mosquito-filled afternoon, when the bazillionith truck drove by our "quiet" street, and then two motorcycles zoomed by for the *third* time—again, we were just trying to make it around the damn block—I burst out to Nathan, "I *hate* where we live. I just hate it." I'm sure Lacey could feel my physical and emotional distress through the leash, and it wasn't helping her relax, but I couldn't control it.

We brought her home just three weeks ago, and for the duration of this trip, we left her in the care of friends who live down our street. While she's back in that noisy neighborhood, I am currently sitting at a picnic table under three huge pine trees in the middle-of-nowhere, Montana (the closest town of Ennis is twenty-five minutes away). The sounds I hear: the rushing of a small river down below me, a variety of birds chirping, the wind, the laptop keys moving underneath my fingertips, sometimes my own breath if I take a deep one. The sights: a pond with two tiny islands of shrubbery in the middle, birds diving to the top of the water to eat, thousands and thousands of pine trees covering mountains right in front of me and in the distance, a wooden fence that hints of the one dirt road that comes to this place, yellow flowers dancing in the breeze, rocky cliffs, and a small sign about catch-and-release fly fishing in the pond, which this ranch refers to as "Jinny's Lake." The hard bench against my sensitive, unpadded butt will be the only reason I will eventually get up. As I enjoy this peace, I'm thinking about Lacey, and high sensitivity, and the real estate listing a friend sent me as we boarded the plane here...for five acres. I'm thinking...

The Move
Part I

It all began with that text as we settled onto the plane to Kalispell. Kayla's message read simply, "Here is a house for ya," and included a link. I glanced at the picture. The house had a mountain-lodge-style look with two-story, floor-to-ceiling windows coming together in a big upside-down V at the roof, surrounded by nothing but green grass and trees. The picture was so dramatic, I figured my friend was joking, but I wasn't sure what the joke was...like, "Haha, if only you were rich and fancy, you could get this dream home on five acres."

Despite my assumption that it was a joke, I was bored as I waited for the plane to pull away from the gate, so I clicked on the link and started scrolling. A separate garage apartment (Nathan had been dreaming of his own space for years). A neighborhood pool. Massive porches, including a screened porch off the bedroom. Acreage. Expansive views of the hill country. I texted my friend back and realized she wasn't kidding. Her next message was the contact info for a real estate agent in town she'd recently employed to help them buy a home on twenty-six beautiful acres. We're all—those of us who are sane, at least—trying to get away from *people*. She just wanted for me what she had recently been lucky enough to find for them.

Fast forward three weeks, almost exactly one year after Cayenne's death, and our offer was accepted. What the hell?! I kept trying to allow this not to happen. We had no plan to move any time soon, though we'd wished we could, as we were so desperate to escape to some peace and quiet before there's no more to be found. When we first walked through the home, my realtor, Debbie—who would become a dear friend, and a surrogate therapist—blatantly said, "Soon, this just won't exist. You won't be able to get five acres with a decent home on it." But despite not being ready, not having the funds (not even close!), and some uncertainty about the status/future of our marriage, the universe seemed to keep shoving this house down my throat.

Somewhere in the middle of the whirlwind, we'd learned, even with the massive profit we stood to make on our current home (this was at the peak of an insanely hot housing market), there's no way we'll ever qualify for a mortgage loan…of any amount, really. A banker told me that in no uncertain terms. He said, "Even with your dad as a cosigner, you will *never* qualify…unless you change your life dramatically and get a real job." (My dad had cosigned on our current home, but that was before he retired.) It had something, well—everything, to do with cash/assets not mattering at all—it's all about your income to debt ratio. The income of two writers wasn't gonna cut it. I hung up the phone, shed a few tears, but then thought with some amount of relief, *Ah, we'll finally give up this silly idea and go back to living our just-fine lives in this over-crowded neighborhood that scares our dog. It's what we know. It's home. It's fine.* But my huge-hearted, hugely generous dad wasn't ready to give up. He talked to his bank people and learned we could do this by taking out a loan against his "portfolio" (a very fancy word I rarely have reason to use) that he established when he retired. The monthly payments would actually be less than with our current house. No down payment required. Nobody cared about our income to debt ratio. Hm.

So…we did all the inspections and amendments to the offer; and, here we are, getting ready to put our house on the market. Our home…our beloved home of nine years that we have poured ourselves into, inside and out. Cayenne's home. It's no surprise I came down with an awful cold. I'm depleted. Every day is an impossible list of tasks involving hours of phone calls with urgent decisions to be made, all involving sums of money I've never discussed in my life. I constantly ask myself how it's possible that things have changed so much since Cayenne died. The rock in my gut has me questioning if I can really leave the place where we spent so many years together, where she was so happy, and where she died. (We're keeping the lot next door—the spirit garden, the fire pit, and her grave; otherwise, there's no way I would've even considered this move.) I wake up regularly at 4 a.m. and tell myself, *You can't do this. What are you thinking? This is home. This is no time to move.*

But in the light of day, I know I'm capable of all kinds of change and loss and gain. I know to let go and trust. I'm remembering all of that wisdom the year's animal spirits have shared with me about transitions, freedom, choices, and knowing I don't have to face any of this alone. We didn't go looking for this house. We didn't go looking for Lacey (specifically), either. They were presented to us, like gifts from the universe. To receive the gift, I have to make the difficult choice to give up our home, what we know, and run wildly, like a brave and powerful horse, into the unknown to find a new home. And I'm remembering my own "wisdom" that I reflected on in Galveston—that endings aren't erasers. Leaving this place doesn't negate all of the love and sweat we put into it or any of the moments and memories it holds. I can do hard things (thank you, Glennon Doyle)—but damn, leaving… …saying goodbye…moving—even to a dream property—is really, really, really hard.

Light and Ease
The Move – Part II

Did I mention how hard moving is for somebody who's afraid of change? So hard that I can go from the self-pep-talk of the final paragraph in that last piece to absolute mental chaos within moments. I'm a mess. This year-long journey of mine was supposed to be coming to a peaceful close—one in which I've grieved and grown and found myself—all wrapped up and tied with a big, beautiful bow. Instead I'm facing the biggest trip of them all, a permanent one. I stress an inordinate amount over the pets and their safety and happiness in this new place we're headed. I stress over all the decisions. So many, damn, decisions. I stress over money *a lot*. I'm living almost fully in fears and thoughts about the future—five minutes from now and five years from now. I'm simply unable to tap into the power of the actual now.

Why am I such a child about things people manage to do every day? Where did I get such a low threshold for change and stress? Wherever it came from (I think I'll blame Mom, for no reason whatsoever; it just seems fair to blame moms for our most annoying traits), I don't want to be like this anymore. In doing my *Artist's Way* morning pages the other day (at 5 p.m. when I finally got to it), I wrote that I want to exude light and ease. I want to be *that* kind of person. I want to move through the world—as unpredictable, scary, and sometimes even infuriating as it can be—with this grace I keep talking about, the grace I named our dog after.

Light and ease. Light and ease. Light and ease. I have to laugh at myself every time I think the words. How opposite they are from my true nature. But that's the point of mantras, right? To manifest something—to make it true—by saying it over and over and over? Maybe I should count, and I'll check back in after 100,000 repetitions. We'll see how light and easy I am then.

Homesick
The Move – Part III

Homebody. Homesick. Homeward-bound. Home has always been everything to me (I mean, given the title of this book, and how many times I've used the word "home" within its pages—142 to be exact—that's kind of obvious at this point, but I refuse to employ the over-used phrase, "It goes without saying," because I'm saying it, again and again, because it matters to me). My parents tell me I used to vomit in the car even just heading out for a weekend at our vacation house on Lake Conroe together. As far as I remember, I loved the times at the lake. I guess my body was just experiencing a visceral reaction to going away, to leaving home.

Home for me has meant an actual place and space— it's not "where the heart is"; it's a physical location. In reading about the emotional challenge of moving, I came across a *New York Times* article that refers to home as one's "matrix of safety." Yep…that's it. Home is a refuge, a sanctuary, a hiding place. It's a place where I surround myself with things that "spark joy" and inspire me—art, photographs, even child-hood stuffed animals. It's a place where I can be the little girl I still feel like am, where I don't have to be anything for anyone else, and I don't have to be afraid of anything.

I lived in the same house from the time my mom and dad brought my newborn-self home from the hospital until I left for college. That house means as much to me as any family member, still. I remember the lines, colors, and textures of it well; think of it often; dream (in my sleep) about it often; and would give anything to be able to return to it (I mean as my home. I do drive by it every time I'm in Houston to say hello). In all those years of living in it, I never wanted to leave it for long. I was okay going off to school, less than a mile away, knowing I would return each day to all the things and spaces that made me feel at peace and safe and comfy: The maroon and forest-green paisley sofa in the study, with its dark green walls and wood paneling, where I would lock the door and watch TV while eating Oreos dipped in a glass of milk. My pink room (I would never have chosen the color, but it also didn't bother me until high school when my mom finally gave in and we transitioned to a less feminine "peach"), where I spent countless hours nestled on the carpet doing homework, playing cassette tapes, and dancing in front of the mirror. Our backyard, the swimming pool, the round white dining table where we'd have dinner every night. It was my perfect matrix of safety.

As my parents prepared to (amicably) divorce during my senior year of high school, there was talk of selling the house. I put my foot down. I told them I'd chain myself to the house if they tried to move. Probably because they sympathized with my sadness over the divorce, they humored me, at least until I went off to

Washington University in St. Louis and couldn't follow through on my threat. My first fall break from school was spent packing up my childhood-teenage room. I came down with a relapse of mono while there, meaning I "had" to stay longer than planned. My body was rebelling. It was chaining itself…

After leaving that house, I lived in two dorms, four apartment buildings, two houses (one bought with my first husband, one Nathan's), a farm briefly, a condo, and finally, the home Nathan and I bought together in Wimberley and shared with Cayenne. This was my adult home. I came to know and love *its* lines, colors, and textures. I could walk through it with my eyes closed and not bump into anything. Cayenne was all over it—literally, her hair still rests in nooks and crannies the vacuum can't reach.

And now we're about to move, and I feel homeless already. The new place feels like somebody else's safety matrix, not mine. I don't have any memories there. As I wander the rooms and begin to unpack boxes, I feel like that little girl in the car on the way to the lake…just trying not to throw up.

Reminder
The Move – Part IV

In the middle of the move (which was an extended process for boring reasons to do with fences, floors, closing dates, etc.), back at the old house, I had to call 9-1-1 for the first time in my life. I was loading the car with stuff and heard screaming. I knew my neighbor's grown daughter was living with her, and I knew she had a meth problem. So while I first assumed I was hearing children, when I heard loud and clear, "HELP! Call the police," I ran inside and did just that, assuming the daughter was trying to kill her mom. The scene that ensued was almost humorous, for what used to be an extraordinarily quiet corner tucked in a Wimberley neighborhood—humorous if I didn't think someone might die. I didn't know so many cop cars even existed in our county. They just kept coming, sirens blazing. There were sheriffs walking around with large (tranquilizer) guns, negotiations, then real guns, then an ambulance immediately in front of our house, guns actually fired (by her), and finally they restrained the daughter—who it turns out was screaming at people who weren't there, not her mother—and placed her inside the ambulance. We took a picture of our real estate agent hammering in the FOR SALE sign three feet away from the ambulance, the woman audibly wailing inside.

Maybe moving isn't such a scary idea.

Nightmare Realized?
The Move – Part V

Note: Please remember my general instability during this time. I waffle back and forth from gratitude/relief and absolute dread about fifty-seven times a day...I wrote this in a dread-state.

One of my recurring nightmares, for years and years, takes me through house hunting and moving into a new place. The dreams are often full-length movies in which we see numerous houses (sometimes, we look at ones my brain had created in previous dreams—I recognize the specific rooms), find one, buy it, and start moving. As we transition to the new house, that's when things get dark. Every time, I slowly realize the house is huge, and often old, usually with a bizarre layout. There are so many rooms that I'd been excited about during the hunt, but now I have no idea what to do with them. None of them make any sense. I literally get lost in the house, just about every time, no matter which house I've landed in within the dream. At some point, panic or depression sets in...and then I wake up.

While I regularly dread the darkness of my dream-world, there is nothing like waking up to reality with utter relief and gratitude. It's literally a wake-up call to how *okay* this real life is compared to the hellscapes I create while sleeping. When I'd had these house dreams in the past, I would wake and look around my bedroom, and be overcome with happiness. Ah, the comfort of my *home*. And now, I'm afraid—to my core—that I'm living my nightmare. A $640,000 nightmare. Whether I close my eyes or open my eyes, this is it. There's no relief, no waking up.

After two months of back and forth, we have officially moved to the big house on five acres. It is old and unfamiliar. It's cluttered with boxes and artwork propped against walls that we don't know where to hang. The cats have been uprooted from a life they loved, the only territory they've ever known. Lacey regularly pees in the one carpeted room of the house—my office—due to the anxiety of the newness. I am lost, and I can never return to the only home that would cure my homesickness: Cayenne. For fifteen years, through divorce and other moves and transitions, she was with me. Without her by my side through this, I don't know where I am. I don't know how to fill this space or what to do in this place. Nathan and I are also lost to each other. We can't navigate this big new thing together. Nathan said he feels like an astronaut whose tether to the ship has broken...just floating in space with no hope of rescue.

I do have hope of rescue, though—not from some heroic outside entity, but from within. Surely, this is where I'm supposed to be. This is the space and quiet and natural beauty I've always longed for. I will transform it from a nightmare to a dream. It will become home. I will form memories with Lacey here. I will plant things that will grow for decades. I will come to know that little oak tree in the yard. I will have friends over, and we will fill the air with laughter. I have to believe that home actually isn't a structure in and of itself. It's a feeling that comes from connectivity to loved ones, to the earth, to the divine. It's a grounding. And I'm learning to ground myself, wherever I am. It's hard, but I have to do it…to learn to connect to what is deep and true and real, so that I am always home. When I read the things I wrote at the very beginning of this year, which has now extended past 365 days, I see I knew back then these are the things I'd have to learn. I guess I'm a little slow, and I'm realizing it was pretty silly to think there'd be any kind of true end to this far-from-linear (remembering Colorado's bear wisdom) adventure of mine.

Breakdown
The Move – Part VI

Three days into actually living here, while Francisco—the incredibly talented hard worker who installed the floors, would build the catio, put together the shed, build the porch steps, and more…all while being nothing but kind and trustworthy—was installing a new dishwasher (because the one that came with the house didn't work, it turned out) well into the night, my back went out. That had never happened to me. It was bad. Like, no-way-could-I-move bad. I didn't want Francisco to worry, so I hobbled, holding onto one piece of furniture after the next, out of sight.

Friends kept stating the obvious—that it was my body telling me to slow down. That'd be great if I had a choice! I'd give anything to slow down. I knew what my body was telling me, because my mind was on the verge of going out, too. But my only option was to buy a TENS machine to numb the pain while making constant trips back to the old house to finish packing it up in time for the closing date on it. Every day, from dusk till dawn, Francisco and his friend were outside working on something. Every day, I had to hassle Marco to get his ass over here and finish the fence so Lacey could go outside. He had said it would only take one week. It ultimately took eight. I never knew what strange men would show up, pulling their massive trucks right up to my bedroom window, work for an hour, then rev up their trucks and leave; and then days would go by when nobody would come to work. The endless phone calls and check-writing continued. It was chaos.

All the while, I had the same old deadlines and work responsibilities that simply had to be met. With all that had to get done, I'd basically given up the two things that didn't: eating and exercise. These two things are essential to my mental and physical well-being, yes, but I wouldn't be dropping anybody else's balls by sacrificing them. One afternoon, I was trying to sit down and focus on work for a rare uninterrupted five minutes or so, while Francisco pounded away on the catio. Because of the catio construction, Stoney and Dylan were limited to the indoors, something very new to them, and to Lacey, who—due to the fence fiasco—was also stuck inside all day except for walks. When Stoney would sweetly (everything he does is sweet to me) wander out of the utility room (the cat room) to try to explore the house, Lacey chased him. It kept happening, over and over. Stoney would scurry away with his tail all fluffed up, and Lacey would bound after him, messing up rugs, running into furniture. Then Dylan would wander in. More chasing. I just wanted my boys to be safe. I wanted the chaos to stop. I wanted to work. Lacey wouldn't listen to a word I said. On about the seventh chase, I ran after her and violently grabbed her neck with both hands. I stood above her shouting, "Stop it, Lacey! Just stop it!" I raised my hand, and I almost hit her. I almost hit my dog. Instead, I opened the door to her

189

crate where she gladly retreated from my rage. I went into the living room, and I lost it. I broke. I couldn't breathe. I sobbed and sobbed and heaved, in a ball on the floor. I almost went out to Francisco to ask for help, for a hug. I was so desperate. So sad. *I'd almost hit my dog.* Instead of seeking an inappropriate hug from this very shy man, I opened the fridge, found a beer, and chugged. And I called a friend who was familiar with panic attacks. After a half hour or so, when the shaking and sobbing had abated, I went into the bedroom and sat next to Lacey's crate. I told her how sorry I was…for losing my temper and for not being a better mom. I also admitted I was missing Cayenne, wishing for her gentle, easy companionship. That made me feel almost as awful as my physical over-reaction. I asked Lacey for forgiveness for it all. She came out of her crate and lay beside me, while I wiped away the tears and breathed, and of course, she gave it.

Stoney

As much as I fail, one of my biggest priorities during this tumultuous transition is the happiness and well-being of my three animal children. The stress over it (that I know is pointless and only adds to their distress) is part of what is making this all so tumultuous in the first place.

Dylan is a massive, fluffy, long-haired tabby. He's your stereotypical aloof cat. His needs are simple. I love him, but I don't worry about him. He's quick to adjust.

Stoney is my soul-cat. White with big patches of brownish gray, he looks exactly like the stones Nathan stacks all over our properties. He blends right in when he lounges on those stone walls. The white parts of his fur are frequently covered in a coat of dirt because of how he loves to roll in it. His sharp white teeth are impossibly tiny. His tiny white paws, with tiny pink pads, are my favorite. Along with his tiny pink nose.

He loved Cayenne, and was always content when she was out in the yard with him. He tried to join us on walks, but I didn't like the idea of him wandering that far from home (though I'm sure he did it all the time on his own), so I never let him. His greatest desire in life—outside of all that wandering and hunting and being generally wild—is to be close to me. When I work out in the yard, he stands on my shoes...back

191

paws on one shoe, front paws on the other…and makes biscuits on them. His favorite time of day, just like me, seems to be sunset, when he curls up on my lap by an outdoor fire and we just sit together. Though, now, I have to gather up the boys before sunset and confine them to the catio and house. I miss our fireside snuggles. I imagine he does, too. But I've been warned that the coyotes out here are more aggressive, and they come out at dusk. He hated this new routine at first. HATED it. He still mews anxiously for the first thirty minutes every evening when I lock them in, but he's learned that being close to me for the night is a silver lining of this new indoor living, and he eventually settles into it. Now his hunting is limited to the day times, and he still does quite well. The other day he left a very large headless lizard for me in the library. He used to get into fights with the neighborhood cats, and despite his scrawny stature, he always seemed to "win." At the new place, there aren't nearly as many neighbors, or cats, so much to my relief, there's less fighting. He's both the most adept wild creature and the most gentle, sweet lap-cat I've ever known.

When I hold him, I feel like we are made of the same stuff. He is like Valium to me, and it seems I am to him. We know each other completely. We talk often. I've never known a cat to chat so much—a constant dictation of his thoughts and feelings and needs. (Cats developed meowing solely to communicate with humans. He doesn't talk to Dylan or Lacey, not with noises. This extensive vocabulary he's developed, with hundreds of different variations, is just for us people, just for me.) Sometimes when he's sleeping soundly, he makes little breathy fluttery sounds that are clearly the coos of an angel.

He's had herpes of the eye since before he came to us at ten weeks old. He'd been rescued from a massive feral cat colony that had gotten out of control. The eye always looked "diseased," with various forms of flare-ups at different times, and it's gotten worse over the years. He refuses all efforts to treat it (though there's not much to be done anyway) and I have little scars on my hands and arms to prove it. While it's all relatively superficial, the issues with his eye remind me regularly of his mortality, and I think often about another impending goodbye. Just as with Cayenne, the day his heart stops beating and mine goes on will be the day my heart cracks wide open again, leaving a scar on it forever. A scar I will cherish.

Stoney and Cayenne on my yoga mat

Dream Shifting
The Move – Part VII

I shall
Gather up
All the lost souls
That wander this earth
All the ones that are alone
All the ones that are broken
All the ones that never really fitted in
I shall gather them all up
And together we shall find our home

~ *Athey Thompson*

I have said, with total certainty, for over twenty years that I will someday have my own animal sanctuary. It would be for those most in need—animals who have been sick, abused, or forgotten and deserve a home to live out their lives in peace and comfort. The plan was to eventually buy at least fifty acres and set it all up to be a paradise for goats and/or donkeys and/or horses and/or cats and dogs. I'd need help, including a guesthouse on the property so a caretaker could always be there when we travel, even for a day. It was all I wanted to do, my ultimate purpose. And when I say I'm going to do something, I do it. It's one of few hard-and-fast values I have.

Then we bought this house on five acres, with deed restrictions. It all happened so fast, in part because of the realization that this may be our only chance at any land whatsoever. At some point during preparations for the move, it hit me: I'm not going to have my own sanctuary. After a time of panic, I actually felt at ease. I began to shift my dream. This property won't allow for a sanctuary, and I'm not likely to get anything "bigger and better." This is it. This is as good as it gets…and it's very good. I began to think of all the ways I can help animals that suit my strengths and lifestyle much better than starting a non-profit, raising funds, managing people, waking at dawn to care for the animals, and being tied to home or employing a caretaker.

As I began to dream this new dream, it felt like a load off, rather than a failure, which is how I usually feel if I don't follow through on a goal or plan. But I didn't fully let it go until I remembered an exchange with an employee at the greatest animal sanctuary on Earth (Best Friends, of course). We'd spent much of my volunteer shift at Horse Haven discussing our mutual lifelong love of animals and our own personal experiences with them. When I expressed uncertainty that I'd ever be able to follow through on my dream, she'd given me very firm advice that I didn't fully appreciate until now. She said, "You don't want or need your own sanctuary. That's running a business. And there are enough sanctuaries and rescue groups to help. Running one is not the path you want to take." She didn't really know me, but she'd listened to me, and she delivered this feedback with such conviction. I now realize she's right; it's like she granted me permission to let go of this idea I'd held onto so tightly that it'd become part of my identity…even as it remained nothing but an idea.

When I formed that idea, that dream, there was so much I didn't know. I had no idea I'd become a writer, who just might use the stories of animals and all of the good people who do good things for them (as well as all of the ways we fail them), to spark a bit of extra compassion among us, to better care for each animal who crosses our individual paths, perhaps someday reducing the need for so many sanctuaries. The ultimate dream is to create a world in which all these animals don't need to be rescued from the cruelties and neglect of humans. And we can all participate in bringing that dream to fruition by increasing our awareness, opening our eyes and hearts, and embracing the fact that we share this planet—this home—with an amazing variety of creatures great and small, each one a life that matters as much as the next. We're just the only creature with the power to destroy this home…or to save it. My property may be small, but my dream has become infinite in size.

Asses It Is

Letting go of the plan to have an actual 501c3 non-profit animal sanctuary does not mean I won't be rescuing animals for the rest of my life. As I've pondered these five acres, the unfortunate limitations of a POA, and my own limitations (mostly financial, some to do with my love of sleeping in), I've wondered what type of animal to devote this mini-refuge-to-be to. A seed had been planted when I visited with a bonded group of four miniature donkeys back at Best Friends—there was something so peaceful about being among them. I'd never thought much about donkeys, outside of Eeyore being my favorite Winnie-the-Pooh character.

It had always been horses for me. I've wanted a horse most of my life. I used to wake up every Christmas morning—in my suburban home in the middle of Houston—and peek out back, by the pool, wishing to see a horse with a big red bow around her neck. I figured she could live out there in the yard, and I'd ride her down the sidewalk to school. Every year that it didn't happen, I lost a bit of faith in Santa. Eventually I came to understand the reality of owning a horse without land or a stable—boarding costs being the tip of the iceberg. And once I moved to Wimberley, where so many people have horses, and I've been lucky enough to befriend some of them so I'm able to ride often...I learned even more about what horses require—time, extensive and know-ledgeable training, veterinary care, lots of expensive food. I hate to do horses the disservice of comparing them to boats, but I decided it's one of those things…it's better to have a friend with a horse.

So I was left wondering about sheep, goats, llamas, alpacas, and donkeys—all of the animals I see daily as I drive around the Hill Country. Donkeys just kept insisting themselves upon me; in asking around, the consensus was that they were super low maintenance, "durable," affordable to feed because they can survive on air, and of course, adorable. I dabbled online, casually checked out a couple of rescue groups, and before I knew it, I was put in contact with a couple who was fostering four donkeys through Blue Moon Sanctuary up in Georgetown, Texas. The idea was for the foster person to just give me some advice about all the stuff I'd need to do on our property to prepare to *someday* adopt donkeys. But she began to send me photo after photo, along with stories of the four: a mama and baby, and a bonded pair of jennies: Pepper and Molly. They'd been rescued from a kill pen, both very young, very sick, and pregnant. They both lost their babies. They were not little Eeyores (I came to learn miniature donkeys are not often available for adoption because people don't "throw them out" like they do standard donkeys), but they were so petite, it was hard to believe they qualified as "standard." When I saw the pictures of them, a switch went off inside me. They lit me up. And that was that. Asses it is. Pepper and Molly to be exact: Ashley's Asses. There is money to be raised, and fences and shelter to be built, but they are there, patiently waiting for me. Waiting to come home.

Cayenne would have loved donkeys. She loved all creatures and had zero predatory instinct. She used to play with deer through the backyard fence, but in her older years, she didn't even register them. Lacey, on the other hand, reacts to every creature—even a tiny bug crawling in the dirt. She sees deer every day of her life and yet, somehow, every time is like the first. If we're walking, she turns to try to bite her leash off, squeals, and jumps, desperate to run to them. I can't tell if she thinks she's a deer and wants to run with them, or if she wants to run *at* them and then eat them. All this is to say, I don't know how she'll respond to donkeys. When the time comes, I'll just have to ask angel Cayenne to visit Lacey and sprinkle some of her magic gentle fairy-dog dust on her.

Donkey

The first thing that comes to mind for most when you mention donkeys is stubbornness. But anyone who makes the effort to actually get to know or understand the species will tell you they're not stubborn—they're intelligent; they're survivors. They need to assess new people, terrain, items, and experiences before just acquiescing to something that may not be in their best interest. When faced with potential danger, they freeze—taking their time in order to listen to their intuition, which they seem to trust beyond any outside entity. Pretty wise, if you ask me.

Largely because donkeys' origins are in desert areas, they're associated with strength and smarts (two qualities a creature needs to thrive in the desert). As they were domesticated about 4,500 years ago, and used by humans for work, they also came to represent faith and being of service. They have a very distinctive bray, one that is most difficult to ignore, which symbolizes one's ability to speak up and be heard. Their large ears can pick up distant sounds, and they know the meaning of the sounds they hear…showing us how to listen, too.

The donkey inspires those who want to be of service in their own unique way, *to create something wonderful and then share it with others.* They represent *undying faith in the creative force—a deep dedication to the universe, to All That Is.*

Stories of specific donkeys abound in literature, including the Bible. While I'm not really into the Bible, it does have a lot of good stories, and it holds my favorite one about a donkey. The gist of it is that a character Balaam sets out on a journey on his ass. God had given Balaam direct instructions *not* to go on this journey, as the objective of it was to put a curse on the Israelites. But he was pressured by his fellow humans to follow through with what they were asking of him. So God let him know he could go ahead, but to listen along the way, because God would tell him what to do and say upon arrival…rather than providing this not-so-nice curse on a mass of people. While riding his donkey, an angel of the Lord appears to avert Balaam's path, but Balaam can't see the angel. The ass sure can, so over and over, she refuses to move forward, and over and over, Balaam beats and punishes her. Until finally, the donkey speaks, in human language—the only animal other than a serpent to speak in the entire Bible. She asks him what she did to deserve his distrust and beatings, and questions whether she'd ever given him reason to doubt her. He is then able to see the angel for himself.

It's obvious why I love this story. The donkey allows him to see the angel. It seems to me that these two rescue donkeys are just the spirit guides I need. I believe little Pepper and Molly will help me *create something wonderful*, as they inspire deep listening, intuitive knowing, and my connection to All That Is. They just might allow me to see angels.

The End...and the Beginning

Moving—perhaps one of the most dramatic forms of travel—extended "Ashley's year of travel" by many months. And now, finally, it's time to officially close the curtain on the year. Here in late December, two months after the move, I can say that I am home. I'm still nesting in this physical space, and within myself. That will likely never end. I still miss our other home. I still miss her, and I know that will never end, but there is no pain associated with the missing.

This "year" has been brutal in many ways. The move was a massive detour in what was already a messy route, not at all resembling a nice, neat straight line from point A to point B. I got very lost. Nathan and I both did. Coincidentally, during the exact same months we were moving, Nathan had to—thanks to the demand of an older brother—devote his time and energy to moving his parents from their beloved home of fifty years (in Oklahoma) to a soulless senior living facility forty-five minutes from us. Nathan's (necessary) preoccupation with all that led this whole moving thing to be an isolating experience—not the peaceful solitude and silence I've been learning to revel in, but a sad, scary, stressful kind of isolation. This last big "trip" may have felt like a few leaps backward on my voyage to find grace, home, and peace within myself...but maybe it was actually just a big fat reset. I feel as though I've been stripped down, and am now starting to reclothe, to rebuild, to reimagine.

Nathan and I are re-imagining our relationship, and I have no idea what that will look like. Some amount of letting go and setting free will be required in order to love both ourselves and one another in the best way. As a human/animal family, we're all having to re-imagine spaces, boundaries, and places within the "pack." The cats have to accept some new rules (being inside more), Lacey has to accept that this is their home too, and I have to accept that no matter how hard I try to keep him safe, Stoney might be killed by a predator out on that acreage, because as much as he loves to be near me, his home is also where the wild things are. And someday soon we'll be adding two sweet rescue donkeys to this family that is little and broken—but still good...yes, still good...as I re-imagine what a sanctuary is. I may not be starting a non-profit, but I am providing refuge, love, and safety for myself, two cats, a dog, and two donkeys who deserve the perfect (however imperfect) home.

No matter how it all turns out, this year has been about learning to have faith—in what I cannot see, and in myself. I've come to know that I am okay, all the time, no matter what, because I'm part of a wondrous universe in which threads of love and energy connect us all, including angels. And I'm more than okay because I'm blessed enough to carry the sparks of Cayenne in my heart. I will keep looking and listening beyond the fear and unknowing, trusting that what I will find is a peace and beauty beyond imagination. I will embrace the moments of sadness and pain, as I look back through these pages at all those moments that felt unbearable, and recognize that I'm still standing, still shining my light...a light that can only be born from within, even if all the love from without helps it to grow brighter. When I open my eyes each morning, I will commit to gratitude...always taking the first moments to sit with Lacey on the floor while she stretches and I scratch her ears and rub her belly, and I will recite our daily mantra: "Laced with grace, Lacey! Let's have a day that is laced with grace, my beautiful girl." And off we'll go...

Lacey and I at Best Friends in 2022

Dear Cayenne,

You died on August 28, 2020, and this year of mine—of ours—comes to an end now, well over 365 days later. Who's to say that a year is a certain number of days…time is an illusion, after all. You, of course, understand the non-existence of time better than I do. Plus, one of the gifts this year bestowed was to remind me how much I love to travel. I don't quite have the financial luxury to continue to traipse around staying at Airbnbs whenever I feel like it. But I plan on going on new adventures whenever I can. Soon I hope to take Lacey up Reservoir Hill in Pagosa Springs, where you, Nathan, and I hiked so many times…you always eagerly pulling me along. I know she'll love it there, too. The travel will go on. The searching will go on. New loves and new losses…really, there is no end.

Thank you for bringing Lacey to me. I knew having another dog, and coming to know the details of her, would make it harder to remember the details of you—your smell, your sounds, how you moved—and it breaks my heart a little. But it's okay. I remember your essence, and I feel as close to you as ever. And I feel you in her sometimes. She's an extremely unique, beautiful dog, so different from you in many ways. I know she'll have very different lessons to teach me, at this very different time in my life. Recently, I left town for the weekend, wearing my "C" and pawprint necklace that I'd not once removed for the 365 days after your death. When I came home, Lacey was so excited to see me, she couldn't help but hug me with her front paws, and in her enthusiasm, she broke the necklace. The discs fell to the floor. I immediately felt the symbolism in this moment. I'd been holding on to the memory of you—of us—a little too tightly. I think Lacey deserves for me to be more present with her, to open up to our special bond and allow her to enter that space in my heart that has so long been yours alone. I got online and ordered an "L" and a new chain from the company where my best friend had found this gift for me, all that time ago. Now I wear a necklace over my heart with a pawprint in the middle and a "C" and "L" on either side.

Thank you for protecting us all, for being our guardian angel. Thank you for sending me rainbows. Thank you for showing me how to believe in magic again. I am so much better because you were in my life. And I'm better because of my grief. My intuition is stronger, my faith abundant. I'm confident that even though I will most certainly get lost from time to time, I'll always find my way back home again.

I love you, sweet angel. Always. Infinitely.

Love,
Mom

Author Bio

Ashley Brown is a writer, editor, and animal welfare advocate. Her first book, *Letters to the Daughter I'll Never Have*, was runner-up in the San Francisco Book Festival competition, Foreword INDIES Finalist, and received an Honorable Mention from the New York Book Festival. She writes and edits for a myriad of publications and works with individual authors as a freelance editor. Ashley lives in the Texas Hill Country with her family of rescues: author and musician Nathan Brown, two cats, two donkeys, and Lacey dog.

MEZCALITA
PRESS

An independent publishing company
dedicated to bringing the printed poetry,
fiction, and non-fiction of musicians who
want to add to the power and reach
of their important voices.

Printed in the USA
CPSIA information can be obtained
at www.ICGtesting.com
LVHW040831290823
756531LV00005B/240